SOUTH WALES VALLEYS SERIES

Railways and Industry in the
TONDU VALLEYS

Ogmore, Garw and Porthcawl Branches

SOUTH WALES VALLEYS SERIES

Railways and Industry in the
TONDU VALLEYS

OGMORE, GARW AND PORTHCAWL BRANCHES

JOHN HODGE & STUART DAVIES

PEN & SWORD
TRANSPORT

AN IMPRINT OF PEN & SWORD BOOKS LTD.
YORKSHIRE - PHILADELPHIA

First published in Great Britain in 2019 by
Pen and Sword Transport

An imprint of Pen & Sword Books Limited
Yorkshire - Philadelphia

ISBN: 978 1 52672 659 9

Typeset by Aura Technology and Software Services, India
Printed and bound in India by Replika Press Pvt. Ltd.

Pen & Sword Books Limited incorporates the imprints of Atlas, Archaeology, Aviation, Discovery, Family History, Fiction, History, Maritime, Military, Military Classics, Politics, Select, Transport, True Crime, Air World, Frontline Publishing, Leo Cooper, Remember When, Seaforth Publishing, The Praetorian Press, Wharncliffe Local History, Wharncliffe Transport, Wharncliffe True Crime and White Owl.

For a complete list of Pen & Sword titles please contact

PEN & SWORD BOOKS LIMITED
47 Church Street, Barnsley, South Yorkshire, S70 2AS, England
E-mail: enquiries@pen-and-sword.co.uk
Website: www.pen-and-sword.co.uk

Or
PEN AND SWORD BOOKS
1950 Lawrence Rd, Havertown, PA 19083, USA
E-mail: Uspen-and-sword@casematepublishers.com
Website: www.penandswordbooks.com

CONTENTS

ACKNOWLEDGEMENTS

We are grateful to the following for their help with photographs and information:

Mike Back, Robert Darlaston, Don Gatehouse, Great Western Trust, Kidderminster Railway Museum, Stephen Miles, Museum of Wales, Rowland Pittard, Porthcawl Museum, Stuart Warr and Richard Woodley.

Special thanks to Ray Lawrence for information on collieries and to Tony Cooke for information on layouts, both of which have been used extensively. Thanks also to Gary Thornton for the use of information on Enthusiast Specials from his website.

Every effort has been made to properly credit the photographers concerned with all the illustrations but where this has not been possible, they should contact John Hodge to rectify the situation. (Email: john_hodge@tiscali.co.uk).

CAPTIONS FOR COVER PICTURES

Front Cover Arriving at the end of its journey to serve collieries at Blaengarw with empty wagons from Margam Yard, Tondu-based 4200 Class No. 4251 pulls into the yard, showing the south end of the complex under the control of the signal box located on the extreme left of the picture. (B.W.L. Brooksbank/Initial Photographics)

Back Cover Top On the last day of operation of the Ogmore Valley services on 3rd May 1958, a three-coach auto service, the 1.55pm Bridgend to Nantymoel, passes Ogmore Vale South Signal Box as the train approaches Ogmore Vale station with 4575 Class 2-6-2T No. 5524 in charge. (S.Rickard/J&J Colln)

Back Cover Bottom A two-coach service from Bridgend to Blaengarw stands in the sun at Blaengarw station waiting to return with the 4pm service back to Bridgend on 28th September 1951 with 5700 Class 0-6-0PT No. 5797 of Tondu, the stock still in the former GWR chocolate and cream. (Gerald T. Robinson)

PREFACE

This is a continuation of the study of the Tondu Valleys, completing each of the railway branches started in the first volume dealing with the Llynfi Valley. Though the correct spelling of Llynfi is with an F, the name became anglicised to Llynvi in the course of time as Welsh single F is pronounced V and it is spelt as such by the railway thereafter. Additionally, we present a photographic record of Enthusiast Specials, Main Line Diversions and two pictorial Chronologies taken on 3 May 1958 when services on the Ogmore Valley were withdrawn and on 7 July 1962, mainly featuring the photographs of Sid Rickard, the well-known South Wales Valleys photographer, who travelled on the Tondu to Porthcawl service that day to record the working.

The first volume, dealing with the Llynfi Valley, also provides full information on the South Wales coalfield as it existed in the whole of the Tondu Valleys as well as full details of the working throughout the Tondu Valleys from Tondu Depot.

Note: In line with standard GWR practice, all trains running from Paddington were described as Down trains and all to Paddington as Up. This also applied to GWR-operated South Wales Valleys services. This varied from the pre-Grouping South Wales companies which (equally logically) described those trains going up the Valleys as Up and coming back down as Down. As the Tondu Valleys were operated by the GWR from an early date, trains proceeding from Bridgend to Cymmer Afan were Down services.

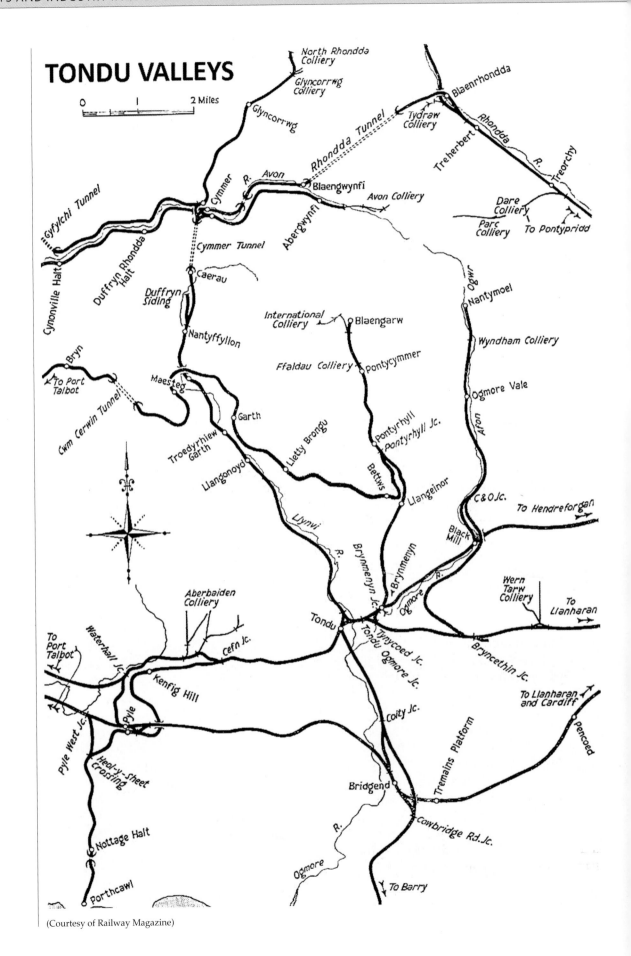

(Courtesy of Railway Magazine)

CHAPTER 1

OGMORE BRANCH

TONDU

North of Tondu station, there was a four-way split; to the south, the lines diverged for Bridgend and Porthcawl, while to the north they diverged between the Llynfi route and that to the Ogmore and Garw Valleys which swung away to the right on a sharp curve.

A drawing for 1875 shows the original engine sheds for the Llynvi Valley Railway and the Ogmore Valley Railway still separate but with their amalgamation and absorption by the Great Western Railway (GWR), a new depot was opened at Tondu in 1889 in the triangle between the Llynfi and Ogmore routes, by when the GWR had completed a triangle of lines with a line linking both routes along the top of the triangle.

The line from Tondu to the Ogmore & Garw Valleys and the branch to Llanharan were under the control of Tondu Ogmore Junction SB, 15ch. from the junction at Tondu Middle. The box stood just north-east of the river bridge crossing the River Llynfi and was opened when the new layout in that area was developed in 1892, though there was a previous box south of the river which was displaced by the new box.

Tondu Ogmore Yard on the north side of the engine shed was created in 1892 as part of the GWR re-planning of the Tondu Triangle, when the original private company facilities were removed. It consisted of nine stop-blocked and five looped sidings. This became the main marshalling yard at Tondu, used as the supply yard for all empty minerals to the collieries in the area and for marshalling loaded traffic into trains for main line destinations. Several other smaller yards

existed; Velin Vach and Tondu Middle between and alongside the platforms at Tondu station and Tondu South on the line towards Bridgend. All were used for holding loaded and empty wagons, as well as coaching stock.

A resident pilot engine served the yard and marshalled inwards and outwards traffic. With the opening of Margam Yard and the introduction of block train working with 21ton Minfits from 6th March 1958, the need for marshalling was reduced and trains were able to run direct from collieries through to Port Talbot Steelworks. Marshalling of wagons of domestic coal especially from Maesteg Washery and Garw Colliery, which supplied domestic coal across South Wales, was still required and the yard remained functional until the opening of the new Margam Yard with its hump-shunting facilities, when a large percentage of the work carried out at Ogmore yard was transferred there. Activities in the area were much affected by this and introduction of dieselisation leading to the closure of the engine shed in April 1964. The running lines between Tondu North and Ogmore Junction were relegated to sidings in 1967. All the sidings on the north side of the Triangle were taken out of use in October 1968, being recovered by July 1969.

Ynysawdre Junction An 1875 drawing shows a trailing connection at Ynysawdre Jct. into Ynysawdre Colliery, owned by Cory Brothers of Cardiff, on the east side of the line. Opened before 1875 and known also as Adare Colliery, it first consisted of two pits – the main shaft and a return (or air) shaft. The main Cribbwr Fawr seam had an average thickness of 5 feet and was a general

A view of Tondu Ogmore Junction SB on 1 July 1961. The eastern corner of the Tondu triangle was at Ogmore Junction where the Signal Box dated from 1892 when the area was redeveloped. It controlled access onto the Llanharan Branch and into/ from the locomotive depot (line on extreme left) as well as the Ogmore/Garw Branch to Brynmenyn. The bracket signal indicates routes for Bridgend (left) and Margam (right). (Michael Hale/GW Trust)

purpose coal. By about 1890, a battery of coke ovens had been added, shown on the 1897 drawing as almost reaching the Ogmore & Garw line, 50 ovens being involved, feeding on small coal brought from the Ogmore & Garw collieries and the Boddwr Fawr Vein, an attached surface outcrop. The coke ovens closed in about 1900, the colliery having closed in 1898. In 1915, slants or drifts were built alongside the old pit reaching the coalface but the yield of coal was very small due to problems affecting the old workings with flooding and the project was abandoned in 1918. (Source *Welsh Coal Mines* – Graham Richards).

The original Ynysawdre Jct. Signal Box (SB) had opened in 1877 on the south side of the line but was replaced in 1892 by a larger box which lasted until 1911 when its functions were taken over by Tondu Ogmore Jct. to the south and Brynmenyn Jct. to the north. Ynysawdre Jct. was the point at which the single branch from

Llanharan joined the Ogmore & Garw line to run south to Tondu, the branch being first opened in May 1877 and completed to Llanharan in 1892. A chord from Brynmenyn to a new junction and associated signal box at Tynycoed was added in November 1892, affording direct running principally from the Garw branch to Cardiff. By 1915, the south face of the triangle proceeding to Tondu had been doubled but the north face had been reduced to sidings, now disconnected from the Llanharan branch and known as Tynycoed Sidings, lasting until the end of 1966.

The Llanharan branch was truncated at Wern Tarw (Raglan Sidings) from 3 December 1962, serving the Wern Tarw Colliery. Following closure of the pit, a large opencast site was developed lasting until 1984 when the remainder of the branch was closed in April. Tondu Ogmore Junction SB was not finally taken out of use until 8 October 1993.

A close-up of Tondu
Ogmore Junction
SB on 15 June 1964.
(D. Wittamore/Kidderminster
Railway Museum)

**Tondu Ogmore
Junction** looking
towards the Loco shed
16 September 1962.
(Michael Hale/GW Trust)

5243 on 22 February 1964, just two months before steam ended at Tondu on 20 April, showing the 42XXs doing what they did best. 5243, in pouring rain, heads a block train of Ogmore or Garw Coal for Margam through the Down Porthcawl Platform. Block Train working (the whole train's origin and destination were the same) had been introduced on 19 February 1962. (RCTS)

22 February 1964 and 4283 with another block train of coal for Margam is held at Tondu Middle's Home Signal waiting the road (Right Hand Bracket Signal for the Down Porthcawl). When introduced, these trains were known as Jumbos by the Tondu Staff. (RCTS)

22 February 1964 and 5243 heads through Tondu Middle Junction with a train of empties for weekend stabling and is about to take the right hand fork towards Tondu Ogmore Junction. The train consists of 21Ton Mineral wagons fitted with continuous brake (Minfits), each of which is stencilled 'To work within South Wales and Monmouthshire Only'. (RCTS)

22 February 1964 and a classic scene of freights meeting at Tondu Middle where 5243 now passes the patiently waiting 4283 on turn D01, bound for Margam with Tondu Shed (home to both) alongside. 4283 would have been held at this point in order to keep Tondu Middle Junction clear. The loop on the Porthcawl branch would have been of insufficient length to accommodate either train. With the introduction of Block Train working at Tondu in 1962 the traditional Tondu 'U' Targets were re-placed with 'D'. (RCTS)

BRYNMENYN JUNCTION

Brynmenyn Jct. was the point at which the Garw Valley line diverged from the Ogmore Valley line.

The 1875 plan of Brynmenyn shows a triangular shaped platform with the double line from Tondu ending at Brynmenyn Junction SB south of the station and becoming two single lines serving the two branches with a diamond crossover to and from the double Tondu route. The station platforms were in the V between the diverging lines and there was a trailing siding off the Ogmore route back alongside the Ogmore platform. On the Garw route, there was a Level Crossing (LC) north of the platform and a loop siding known as the Weighbridge Siding beyond on the north side of the single line branch line.

A small Brynmenyn Colliery was opened in 1895 and embraced the weighbridge siding, by when all collieries in the area would have possessed their own weighbridge. When the pit was opened in 1895 by J.T. Salafield, it only employed 11 men; in 1906, when taken over by Soloman Andrews & Sons of Cardiff, it employed 32 men and this rose to 151 by the time the colliery closed in 1910. Fireclay was mined with the coal and this was probably used in the local brickworks. Later attempts to re-open the colliery in 1927/8 failed due to the many faults in the underground working and the amount of water flooding in, requiring constant use of pumping machinery. The original weighbridge loop siding was sold to the GWR when the colliery closed and remained in use until taken out in 1965.

By 1897, the double line from Tondu had been extended into the station at Brynmenyn and double platforms of equal length had been provided. Beyond the

A lovely 1921 shot of a Tondu 2721 class saddle tank No. 2734 in the yard with a container from or bound for Bristol. (Stephenson Locomotive Society)

A quality view of the junction at Brynmenyn, probably in the 1920s. The Garw branch is on the left and the Ogmore on the right with the 'Y' shaped centre platform, shared between both. Note the LC at the north end of the Garw branch platforms. (Lens of Sutton)

platforms, the lines became single and were slewed in the case of the Ogmore platform to accommodate the trailing siding. This was taken out of use in August 1965, as was a siding approaching the station from the south. The Brynmenyn Crossing SB controlling the LC at the north end of the Garw platforms was closed in 1907 and covered by a Ground Frame (GF).

Ogmore Valley trains from Bridgend to Nantymoel normally (except Saturdays) conveyed a rear portion for Blaengarw which was uncoupled just south of Brynmenyn Junction SB and was then taken forward by a fresh engine waiting at the station to reverse onto the portion. In the reverse direction the Garw service arrived first, engine uncoupled and ran clear, the incoming Ogmore Valley train, having completed station duties, ran

forward and reversed onto the Garw coaches which it then attached rear for the onwards journey to Bridgend. The Garw branch passenger service was withdrawn in 1953.

In 1965, whilst retaining the actual junction at Brynmenyn, the entire layout was singled on both the Ogmore and Garw branches. Then from October 1968, the two running lines north of Tondu Ogmore Jct. were made bi-directional, the former down line serving the Garw Valley and the former up line the Ogmore. Thus, Brynmenyn ceased to be a splitting junction for the two routes, dispensing with the junction and signal box, with the Ground Frame for Brynmenyn Crossing lasting until August 1973, when the crossing gates were converted for traincrew operation.

The actual junction at Brynmenyn preceded the station which as a result was located in its 'V' with loops on both the Ogmore and Garw branches, each line having a platform (four in total). The Garw portion of trains was uncoupled by a Porter/Shunter and then left outside the station (as can be seen just by the Signal Box) to be collected by the branch engine when the main train had drawn forward into the Down Ogmore platform as seen here with 3695 on 2 August 1951. (R.C. Riley/Transport Treasury)

Running into the Garw Valley platform at Brynmenyn on 2 August 1951, 9660 with a two-coach service from Bridgend to Blaengarw. (R.C. Riley/Transport Treasury)

Brynmenyn on 28 September 1951, with 5797 on its two-coach service from Blaengarw (left) and 7770 on a similar two coach train from Nantymoel (right). For services on to Bridgend, the branch (Garw) service arrived first, its engine was detached and moved clear, allowing the Ogmore portion, when its station duties were complete, to draw forward, reverse into the adjoining platform and couple-up to the branch train. On arrival at Bridgend, the two portions would be at the wrong end to return to the valley they had just arrived from. To compensate for this, it was necessary for both the Ogmore and Garw portions to consist of the same number and type of vehicles and thus be capable of alternating between the two services. (Gerald T. Robinson)

A Bridgend to Nantymoel two coach service, powered by 7770, stands at the Ogmore Valley platform at Brynmenyn on 28 September 1951, with empty mineral wagons standing alongside in the station siding. (Gerald T. Robinson)

Standing at the up Garw platform in 1951, 3772 with its two-coach service from Blaengarw to Bridgend. Though there is no up Ogmore service in the picture, the crew have time to stand around, perhaps awaiting its arrival and the joining-up procedure. (SLS)

Looking south from Brynmenyn Junction towards Tondu Ogmore Junction on 5 April 1958, when all running lines and sidings were mostly still intact. However, in 1940 the line diverging left on the left-centre of the picture and previously linking into the Tondu to Llanharan branch at Tynycoed Jct., was truncated before that junction to become sidings and the two running tracks reduced to one, linking only into the down main line on the Garw & Ogmore line as can be seen. Running south on the down side as far as Ynysawdre Jct. (the junction with the Llanharan-Tondu line) was a nest of sidings, here full of EMWs, which were laid in during the 1920s and taken out of use in May 1975. The whole of the layout from Tondu was ultimately reduced to two single lines, one to each Valley before complete closure. (Michael Hale/GW Trust)

Looking north from the north end of the up Ogmore Valley platform at Brynmenyn, 6416 heads for Nantymoel with a three-coach auto SLS special on 2 July 1960. (Stephenson Locomotive Society)

Brynmenyn Junction viewed on 6 August 1963. (Garth Tilt)

Brynmenyn Junction on 6 August 1963 taken from the Island Platform looking towards Tondu. (Garth Tilt)

Brynmenyn looking north on 18 July 1967. The two Ogmore & Garw lines have been singled from Tondu Ogmore Jcn. with an actual junction retained at Brynmenyn, albeit a very simple one. (Lens of Sutton)

A second view on the same day showing the main station building and waiting shelter still in existence on the Down Garw Platform, eight years after the last passenger train had served Brynmenyn. (Lens of Sutton)

The former Brynmenyn Signal Box, here on 20 April 1985, remained for the use of the Level Crossing Keeper until the latter became Traincrew Operated. The Ogmore & Garw branches had been remodelled as two separate running lines from Tondu and the junction at Brynmenyn was no more. (Garth Tilt)

BLACKMILL

Blackmill stood at 2m 55ch. from Brynmenyn Jct. and here the track again forked, the western fork for Cardiff & Ogmore Jct., Ogmore Vale and Nantymoel and the eastern fork for Hendreforgan and Gilfach Goch.

The 1875 plan shows a simple junction and a triangular platform with a long loop running north of the Ogmore line (added by 1881) and a trailing south facing connection into a stop-blocked goods yard and shed, well north of the station. There was a similar long loop also added in 1881 on the Hendreforgan branch from the junction to north of the platform.

By 1897, the platform on the Ogmore branch had been considerably lengthened, together with both loops and sidings provided at the junction for each branch, further lengthened in 1910 on the Ogmore side and in 1923 on the Hendreforgan. The station had a platform face on one loop of each branch only. To enable trains in opposite directions to cross on either branch, both branch loops were signalled for bi-directional running. However, with only one platform, it was not possible to cross two passenger trains.

Some Bridgend to Nantymoel trains conveyed a rear portion for Gilfach Goch until 1930, when the service ceased. In a similar practice to Brynmenyn, the Gilfach coaches were detached outside the station and collected by the Gilfach engine. In the reverse direction, the Gilfach service arrived first, engine uncoupled and ran clear. The Ogmore train, after completing station duties, drew forward, set back onto the Gilfach portion, attached and then departed for Bridgend. The passenger service from Bridgend to Gilfach Goch which had begun on 24 May 1881 was withdrawn on 22 September 1930 and thereafter the line was used for empty wagon storage, this being itself terminated in 1957 when it was completely closed back to the junction at Blackmill.

A short distance outside Blackmill, the Gilfach Goch branch was crossed by a long viaduct carrying the Bryncethin Jct. to Cardiff & Ogmore Jct. branch of the former Cardiff & Ogmore Railway line from Llanharan, to meet the Nantymoel line at Cardiff & Ogmore Jct. near Lewistown. This line was opened in October 1876 but never realised the developers' intentions of carrying coal from the Ogmore Valley pits to Cardiff and closed in July 1938, being recovered in April 1939.

The Viaduct consisted of two masonry abutments, six masonry pillars and seven lattice steel girder spans. It was opened with the line on 2 October 1876 and built at a cost of £133,300. It skirted the hillside at just under the 350 foot contour, 80 feet above ground level and approximately 332 yards long. It was designed by James Szlumper of Aberystwyth who was later to undertake the Barry Railway's Walnut Tree Viaduct and Llanbradach Viaduct. The route was closed in 1938 having only one scheduled mineral train a day in later years and the viaduct was dismantled on 24 September 1938 but the piers still remain.

January 1964 saw the closure of the Blackmill SB, located on the south end of the Ogmore branch platform and the recovery of all remaining sidings, leaving a plain single line. This remained the case until the whole of the Ogmore branch was closed in 1985.

Blackmill in the early 1930s, possibly with a train from Gilfach Goch, which is still formed of four wheelers with train engine 2736. The occasion must be of some importance as the staff are posed for the picture and could well record the closure of the Gilfach passenger service in 1930. Note the height of the signal box, tall enough to see over the top of the station canopy. (Nevis)

With the 3pm Nantymoel to Bridgend train on 28 September 1951, 7770 calls at Blackmill with its two- coach train. The station nameboard still carries reference to the Gilfach branch though that service ended in 1930. (W.A. Camwell/SLS)

Tondu's 5545 runs into Blackmill with a two coach auto to Nantymoel on 3 April 1958, showing the small canopied waiting area for passengers. (Robert Darlaston)

Two views on the last day of service on 3 May 1958 of 5545 arriving and departing Blackmill with a three-coach auto service from Nantymoel to Bridgend; by now the station nameboard has lost all its lettering. (John Hodge)

Two views of Blackmill on 6 August 1963. The first, looking north, showing the formation of the Gilfach branch on the right with the disused station building and signal box boarded up. The second is taken from the north end of the station on the Ogmore side looking towards Tondu; the siding in the foreground served the former Goods Shed. (Garth Tilt)

At Blackmill, the Gilfach branch was crossed by a long viaduct carrying the Bryncethin Jct. to Cardiff & Ogmore Jct. branch of the former Cardiff & Ogmore Rly's line from Llanharan to meet the Nantymoel line at Cardiff & Ogmore Jct. (both Author's collection)

General View, Blackmill.

BLACKMILL
1923

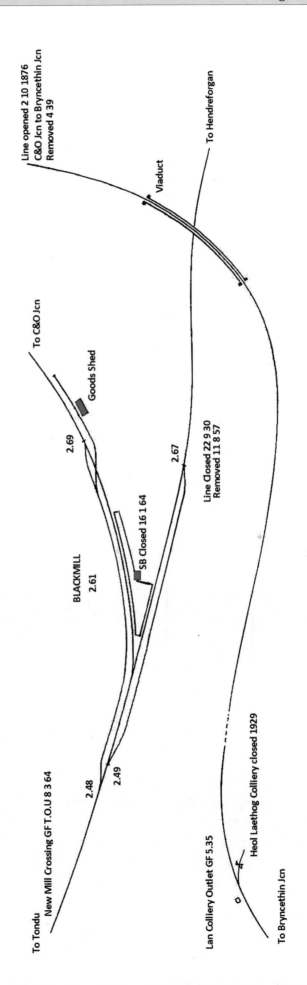

To Tondu

New Mill Crossing GF T.O.U 8 3 64

2.48

2.49

BLACKMILL
2.61

2.69

Goods Shed

To C&O Jcn

SB Closed 16 1 64

2.67

Line Closed 22 9 30
Removed 11 8 57

Line opened 2 10 1876
C&O Jcn to Bryncethin Jcn
Removed 4 39

Viaduct

To Hendreforgan

Lan Colliery Outlet GF 5.35

Heol Laethog Colliery closed 1929

To Bryncethin Jcn

CARDIFF & OGMORE JUNCTION (LEWISTOWN)

This was the point at which the line from Llanharan and Bryncethin Jct. (the original Cardiff & Ogmore Railway) joined the Ogmore Valley branch at 3¾ miles from Brynmenyn Jct., both lines having just crossed the River Ogmore. Between the river bridge and the junction, the line from Bryncethin Jct. was double, but the whole line was closed in July 1938 and when the Cardiff & Ogmore Jct. SB closed, the location ceased to exist. Just south of the junction was Lewistown Halt, opened in 1942 and closed on 4 June 1951.

South of Ogmore Vale was originally Caedu Colliery which became Tynewydd Colliery and was later absorbed into the new Penllwyngwent Colliery. Here was the famous Caedu Incline on which empty curved-bottomed drams can be seen being rope hauled up the incline to Cwm Fuwch Colliery on a time interval basis, the equally spaced empties on the nearer track and the loaded, worked on a similar basis, on the other track. (Ogmore Valley Local History and Heritage Society)

Lewistown Ground Frame viewed on 4 August 1964. This gave access to the south end of Ogmore Central Washery (also known as Rhondda Main). (Garth Tilt)

With Lewistown forming the backdrop, Type 3 Class 37 239 heads towards the Washery with an empty train of 21ton Minfits to load another train for Margam Steelworks on 4 April 1986. (Acton Wells Junction)

A 4 August 1964 view looking up the valley with Caedu Signal Box in the centre distance. The track coming in on the right is the northern access to Ogmore Vale Central washery. (Garth Tilt)

Caedu Signal Box viewed on 20 June 1970 with the traditional gates protecting the level crossing. (Garth Tilt)

OGMORE VALE CENTRAL WASHERY (RHONDDA MAIN COLLIERY)

A plan of the area for 1876 shows only a single line running alongside the River Ogmore where this complex would be developed, crossing the river at the 4¾ mp. In 1909, a Private Siding Agreement (PSA) was taken out by Lewis Merthyr Consolidated Collieries Ltd. for Rhondda Main Colliery on a site north of the single line which was then doubled in 1911. Rhiwglyn SB was opened also in 1911, controlling access to/from the colliery at the south end, the northern access being at Caedu. The colliery itself was only in production for a ten-year period from 1914-24, with records showing there were approx. 700 employed there in 1918 and approx. 1,000 in 1923. It closed the following year, its advantageous position as the most southerly colliery in the Ogmore Valley led to its being converted into a washery to serve all those pits above it in the Valley where a washery was not provided.

On the west side of the double line, at the northern end of the Rhondda Main complex, a siding into the Mary Pits opened in 1923, again owned by the Lewis Merthyr Co. Both Mary Pits and what would have by then been the Ogmore Vale Central Washery passed into the hands of Cory Brothers of Cardiff in 1933. Rhiwglyn SB closed in July 1938 and was replaced by a GF controlling the southern exit from the Washery. Mary Pits closed by 1954 when the PSA was terminated.

A new Central Washery and Coal Preparation Plant opened in January 1959, the principal concern being to produce the blend of prime coking coal (e.g. volatility and caking rating, ash and sulphur content) necessary for Port Talbot steelworks from the Wyndham/Western and Penllwyngwent coals treated there. Here, it joined similarly prepared coals from the Eastern and Western Valley, mostly prepared at Hafodyrynys Coal Preparation Plant where coals from Hafodyrynys itself and from Llanhilleth, Tirpentwys and Blaenserchan were blended together to form prime coking coal.

A plan for 1960 shows the full extent of the Washery with 4/5 loop reception sidings at the north end of the plant, accessed below Caedu, leading to a tippler road where the incoming coal for washing was tipped before processing through the Washery and passing through the screens served by four tracks which then became six sidings at the south end. There was also a GF entry into the reception sidings at the north end, near the tippler, known as Rhondda Main North GF at 4m 49ch and this remained in use until the 1980s. The Washery closed from March to July 1983 for reconstruction and then finally in 1986, the last train of empties (from inward supply) leaving on 20 May.

Initially, the raw coal washed at Ogmore Vale Washery came from only the collieries above Ogmore in that valley, namely Wyndham, Western and Penllwyngwent, but in later years, coal from Garw and Ffaldau Collieries was treated there, despite the long rail trip there via Tondu, making it a very costly product, the National Coal Board (NCB) frequently stating that the railway conveyed twice the amount of coal they produced.

A mile south of Ogmore Vale station was Rhondda Main Colliery which became Ogmore Vale Central Washery, washing and blending all the coal produced in the Ogmore Valley and for a while that also produced in the Garw, largely for use as prime coking coal for Margam steelworks. A trainload of coal for the steelworks in 21ton Minfits leaves Ogmore Central Washery on 14 December 1983. In 1986, the last wagon (B312772) was tipped on 16 May, the last coal was washed on 12 June and the Washery itself was closed on 21 June. Sadly, the last train of reclaimed coal in Merry-Go-Round wagons, hauled by 37 235/251 on 16 July, was refused at Aberthaw Power Station because of its poor quality – an unfitting end!

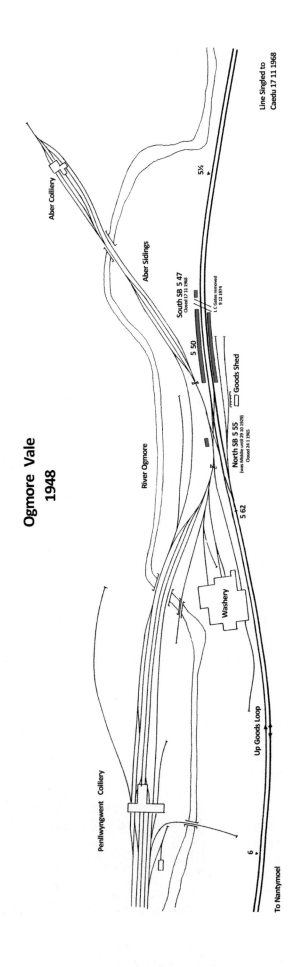

Ogmore Vale
1948

Aber Colliery

Aber Sidings

River Ogmore

Penllwyngwent Colliery

Washery

Line Singled to
Caedu 17 11 1968

5½

South SB 5 47
Closed 17 11 1968

L C Gates removed
9 12 1974

5 50

Goods Shed

North SB 5 55
(was Middle until 29 10 1929)
Closed 24 1 1965

5 62

Up Goods Loop

6

To Nantymoel

OGMORE VALE

Having passed Caedu SB and LC, from where trailing connections accessed Rhondda Main colliery (subsequently Ogmore Vale Central Washery), the railway running north approached Ogmore Vale, just over 5½ miles from Blackmill. Though Caedu SB and LC were south of Ogmore Vale, Caedu Colliery, open from 1865 to 1891, was a mile further north.

The passenger service from Bridgend opened on 12 May 1873 to Tynewydd (renamed Tynewydd Ogmore Vale in 1884 and Ogmore Vale in 1902) consisting of a small single line passenger platform with a LC at its south end. A long loop siding, extending for half a mile, ran alongside the main line on the east side for dealing with traffic from the collieries north of the station. Beyond the platform were connections on the east side of the line into Aber Colliery and on the west side to Caedu and Tynewydd Collieries. Coke Ovens from these collieries were located alongside the single main line, flanked by a siding on each side with the half mile long loop running from No. 2 SB at 6mp (Ogmore Vale North SB from 1892) at the north end of the complex, running past the coke ovens and platform to an outlet onto the single line at 5½mp. Opposite the coke ovens on the north side of the line, were Caedu and Tynewydd Collieries on the west side between 5¾ and 6mp with three loop sidings shown, considerably extended by 1881.

A plan for 1897 shows that the long siding had been converted into an Up Goods Loop in 1892, though the running line was single. The Goods Loop was however used by passenger trains to access the new Up platform when the station was rebuilt in 1892 with two new platforms, a goods shed and yard on the west side. The level of rail activity now required the GWR to open three SBs at Ogmore Vale in 1892, North box, at the very north end of the complex, where the line northward became single again and from where the new Up (southbound) Goods Loop ran through the new Up platform to a new connection into the single running line just past the SB and LC south of the station. The new Up Goods Loop continued south by a train length then feeding into the single line. The new Centre SB was just north of the station controlling access into Aber and Tynewydd Collieries and the Coke Ovens, while the new South box controlled the LC at the south end of the station, located at the south end of the Up platform. In 1911, the double line was extended south to Cardiff & Ogmore Jct.

By a drawing of the layout for 1914, there were no colliery installations on the west side of the line, all activity being confined to the east side, where Penllwyngwent Colliery had been opened in 1912, with most activity at Aber now being the handling of coal from nearby Cwmfuwch. There were seven tracks running into the Penllwyngwent screens from the north end with five at the south end, feeding into two long sidings running down to Middle Box (the previous Centre), from where trailing sidings led to the Washery which had been developed from the previous coke ovens. Middle Box became North Box in October 1929 when the previous North Box was closed. Aber Colliery was closed by the termination of the PSA in April 1939 but the sidings were retained as overflow from Penllwyngwent which closed in 1969. The connections into both pits were taken out of use in 1970. The passenger service had ceased in 1958, coal being the only traffic over the line from that time.

The Up Goods Loop, Goods Yard and Shed were removed in 1964/5 and the line singled back to the junction at Blackmill in November 1968. Single Line operation continued until the closure of Wyndham/Western and Ogmore Valley Central Washery in 1984 when the line north of Brynmenyn was closed.

Collieries

Caedu Colliery, located north of Ogmore Vale was one of the earliest collieries in the area. It was opened in 1865 by John Brogden, working the No. 2 Rhondda seam. It was a drift mine with an upcast ventilation shaft and was linked to the nearby Fforchwen level. Ownership passed to the Llynfi, Tondu & Ogmore Coal & Iron Co. in 1878. This company had been formed in 1872 with a capital of £500,000 to replace the Llynvi Iron & Coal Co. which ran Maesteg Iron Works and other works in the area. Alexander Brogden was the Chairman with Henry Brogden as Managing Director. The trade depression of the late 1870s, coupled with the problems posed by the changeover to steelmaking, forced the company into receivership in 1880. New ownership also failed to make the necessary impact on the state of affairs and in 1888, the pit was bought for £350,000 by a group of businessmen led by Colonel North, the company later becoming North's Navigation Collieries (1899) Ltd. Caedu was noted locally for the Caedu Incline (See photo Page 28) where drams were worked on the gravitation principle from a higher level down to the colliery. The screens spanned three short loop sidings which were extended south and north by 1881. In 1891, the new owners abandoned work on the No. 2 Rhondda seam and the pit closed.

Tynewydd Colliery was in the same area as Caedu and worked the No. 2 and No. 3 Rhondda seams, located about 300ft. below the No. 2. The owners abandoned the No. 2 Rhondda seam in 1901 and the No. 3 Rhondda in January 1905, when it closed. All installations on the west side of the line were then removed and all colliery activity took place on the east side of the line, across the River Ogmore.

Aber Colliery across the river on the east side of the line also appears to have been opened about 1865, owned by Nicholson & Taylor, in 1883 by the Aber Coal Co., in 1886 by the Aber & Ynysawdre Coal & Cole Co., and in 1891 by the Aber Colliery Co., before passing to Cory Bros. in 1896. It was originally a

drift mine accessing the outcrop of the No. 2 Rhondda seam while a second drift, driven in 1886, accessed the No. 3 Rhondda seam. These were prolific seams of 33-42ins and 28-36ins respectively, the mineral take stretching from Nantymoel south to Blackmill. Work on the No. 2 seam ceased in 1894 and activity was concentrated on No. 3. In 1896 when taken over by Cory Bros., 25 men were employed underground and 17 on the surface. This increased in 1899, to a total of 219 and in 1900 321 as the mine was developed. The numbers declined during the first decade of the new century and in 1909 was down to 174 but only 34 in 1911 and only 10 in the early 1920s. It still remained a listed working but was later shown as disused and the Private Siding Agreement with the GWR was terminated in April 1939, all mining activity being centred on Penllwyngwent a short distance to the north.

However, coal raised at the nearby Cwmfuwch drift mine was also processed through Aber Colliery and was actually known as Aber No. 3. This was opened by Cory Bros. in 1901 and consisted of two drifts 25 yards apart, producing house, manufacturing and steam coals from the Nos. 2 and 3 Rhondda seams until 1921 when work ceased on both. Between 1908-19, it often employed around 300 men, though dipped to 198 in 1913. Production ceased between 1923-5 and from then until 1933, there were between 12 and 51 employed but in 1935, it was merged with Penllwyngwent which then replaced it and the No. 3 Rhondda seam was abandoned at Cwmfuwch.

Penllwyngwent Colliery was a short distance north of Aber and was opened by Cory Bros. between 1905 and 1912 to exploit a geological fault in the area which was called the Yard or Bute seam which had a thickness of 66ins. With the Upper-Nine-Feet seam with a thickness of some 54ins. and the Lower-Six-Feet seam of up to 98ins., this made Penllwyngwent a very prolific pit, alongside their

Wyndham pit at Nantymoel. Due to this geological fault, called the Jubilee Slide, all the seams from the Six Feet seam to the Lower-Nine-Feet seam are missing in a belt at least half a mile wide at this mine. The 394 miners employed at the pit in 1913 would be vastly exceeded in future years. In that year Cory Bros. advertised as follows:

<u>Cory Brothers & Co. Limited</u>
Colliery Proprietors and sole shippers of Cory's Merthyr Steam Coal and Penrikyber Navigation Steam Coal Cory Brothers & Co. Ltd. supply all the principal Lines of Steamers and are Contractors to the Governments of Great Britain, Germany, France, Italy, Greece, Austria, Brazil &c.
Head Office Bute Docks, Cardiff.

The colliery produced type 301A Prime Coking Coal for use in steelworks and foundries, making it a leading supplier to the Steel Company of Wales which opened in 1935. Until Nationalisation, the pit employed 145 in 1909, 526 in 1910, 670 in 1923, 820 in 1926, then falling back to first the 700s then the 600s and 500s leading to 1947. In 1948 519 were employed with a production of 110,000 tons and with manpower falling almost each year until 1961 when it was down to 376, production ranged between 108k and 140k with the maximum achieved in 1953. With production down to 82k in 1961, Penllwyngwent was closed by the NCB at the end of February 1969, almost 200 of the miners transferring to the Wyndham/Western pit at Nantymoel.

Between the colliery and the running line a small power station was located opened by Cory Bros. and run by the Ogmore Vale Electric Light & Power Supply Co. (1891-1944).

Ogmore Vale station and South Signal Box still appear capable of handling a passenger service in this view taken on 6 August 1963 despite being withdrawn in 1958.
(Garth Tilt)

St. John's Square Ogmore Vale at the turn of the century. The level crossing was located just south of the station which will be located to the right of the picture. (Ogmore Valley Local History and Heritage Society)

Ogmore Vale SB in 1964. It closed on 17 November 1968. (Lens of Sutton)

Ogmore Vale South
Signal Box, Level Crossing and Up Platform seen from a passing Down train on 2 July 1960. (KRM)

During the 1950s, Tondu had three of the 9400 Class panniers allocated, mainly for passenger working. Here on 12 August 1957, 8497 heads the 3.50pm three coach service from Bridgend to Nantymoel into Ogmore Vale, from where it will depart at 4.15pm on the final stage of the journey. (Ian L. Wright)

A leaky 5545 makes an impressive start southward from Ogmore Vale with a Bridgend auto service on 5 April 1958. Ogmore Vale is the commercial centre of the Ogmore Valley and immediately behind W171W is the Gwalia General Ironmongers Store now preserved at the Welsh Folk Museum at St Fagans. (Michael Hale/ GW Trust)

A view along the down platform at Ogmore Vale on 11 April 1958 with coal wagons in Aber Sidings on the up side of the station as the 2.15pm Nantymoel to Bridgend auto service with 5524 makes ready for departure. (Robert Darlaston)

A view south on 2nd July 1960 towards Ogmore Vale North Signal Box and Aber Sidings access to which was adjacent to the Box and controlled by the two 'ringed' arms to the left of the Main Signals. Of the latter, the Distant for Ogmore Vale South was fixed (non-operational) dictating a maximum speed of 15 mph. Fixed signals were a common GWR feature and applied where boxes were in close proximity or line speed was non-critical avoiding the costs of the associated signal wire provision and maintenance. Aber Sidings were originally used for coal emanating from Aber Colliery but afterwards were retained as an overflow for Penllwyngwent.
(R.S. Carpenter)

Ogmore Vale North on 5 April 1958 as the daily pick-up goods makes its way to Nantymoel, the driver receiving the train staff from the North Box signalman. The Goods Yard is seen on the right, closed in 1964. On the left the lead in the foreground is into Penllwyngwent Colliery while the wagons behind the station are in Aber Sidings. (Michael Hale/GW Trust)

Ogmore Vale North taken on 4 August 1964 looking towards Tondu. A similar view to the previous image which shows how rapidly the scene can change. (Garth Tilt)

Ogmore Vale North looking south on 20 June 1970. The connections to Aber Colliery are seen on the left of the picture. (Hugh Davies collection)

Aber Colliery was located north-east of Ogmore Vale and was accessed from Ogmore Vale North SB. Though Aber ceased production in 1914 when nearby Penllwyngwent opened, coal from nearby Cwm Fuwch Colliery continued to be processed and loaded at Aber Colliery screens and sidings until 1939.
(Author's collection)

The Penllwyngwent Colliery engine, Hudswell Clarke 0-6-0ST No. 618 Antonia of 1902 vintage. (Alan Jarvis)

Standing in for the colliery engine in June 1956 is ex GW 850 Class Pannier 1923. (SLS)

NANTYMOEL

The approach to Nantymoel begins at Wyndham Pits South SB at 6m.41ch. from Brynmenyn. A plan for 1875 shows the single line railway from Ogmore Vale with Wyndham Colliery and associated sidings on the south side of the line with the SB at the south end of the complex on the north side of the line. The colliery was opened in the latter part of 1865 by John Brogden & Sons who also built the railway to carry the high-quality dry steam coals to Porthcawl Harbour. In 1872, ownership of the colliery passed to the Llynfi, Tondu, Ogmore Coal & Iron Co. then to North's Navigation Collieries (1889) Ltd.

On the north side of the line were outlet sidings from the Ocean Colliery of David Davies & Co, for which the first PSA was 1878, which would become the Western Colliery by 1956 when it merged with the Wyndham.

The colliery sidings were much enlarged and extended by 1914. A new SB was provided in 1925 about 12 chains south of the original. A new Up Goods Line was introduced in November 1929, feeding into the Up Goods line at Ogmore Vale. A new Wyndham Halt platform was opened south of the colliery complex in August 1942. The Up Goods line was taken out of use in January 1964 and the SB was replaced by a GF in January 1965. The colliery continued in production until October 1983, ceasing winding on 9th, the last coal train departing on 20th and surplus wagons the next day.

Near the 6¾mp, Wyndham Pits North SB was opened by 1875 on the north side of the line, controlling siding access on the south side. To the north of the line between North SB and the passenger station were tramways of the Ocean Colliery with a loading bank connected to the single main line. Almost at the end of the branch, Nantymoel passenger station, consisting of a single platform, was located at roughly the 7mp, the branch finishing at 7m18ch. A run round loop and a siding at the south

end of the platform were also provided at the station.

A drawing for 1880 shows the outlet sidings from the Ocean Colliery to have been further developed with access to the main line at Wyndham Pits South with 3 sidings shown for outwards loaded wagons while an inlet to the colliery for empty wagons had been provided near the site of the previous loading bank, just south of Nantymoel station. In 1891/2, the Nantymoel passenger platform was extended northwards to accommodate longer trains and the surrounding siding and loop were also lengthened. In August 1899, the PSA for the Ocean Colliery passed from David Davies & Co. to the Ocean Colliery Co.

South of the Wyndham Colliery sidings, a tramway existed under a PSA dated September 1916 to F. W. Loughor & Co. but this was terminated in September 1918.

Wyndham Pits North SB closed by July 1924, movements into the north end of the colliery sidings being controlled by a GF. By May 1946, the PSA for the Ocean Colliery had passed to the Ocean & United National Collieries Ltd. and by 1956 the Ocean Colliery had become the Western Colliery. This closed as a separate entity in May 1972 when it merged with the Wyndham Colliery to become the Wyndham Western. This became the most prolific mine in the South Wales coalfield and was to last until 1984, its produce all being washed at the Ogmore Vale Central Washery via an underground link.

Nantymoel station and the whole of the Ogmore Vale passenger service closed in 1958. Nantymoel SB closed in January 1964 when the lines beyond the previous SB were all taken out of use.

The branch was truncated at Ogmore Vale South in 1983, following closure of Wyndham Colliery and remained purely to handle coal from the Garw Valley for washing at Ogmore Vale Central Washery. When this ended with the usual reclamation of tips etc. in 1985, the line down to Brynmenyn closed completely.

Between Ogmore Vale and Nantymoel was Wyndham Halt which afforded transport to miners at Wyndham Pits and also to the many houses which can be seen behind the halt, most occupied by miners at the several local collieries. In this view 5545 heads the 9.30am train into Nantymoel on 5 April 1958, a month before service closure. (Michael Hale/GW Trust)

A view of Wyndham Halt looking towards Nantymoel on 6 August 1963. The Up Line is clearly out of use and the Halt closed in May 1958 with the withdrawal of the Passenger service. (Garth Tilt)

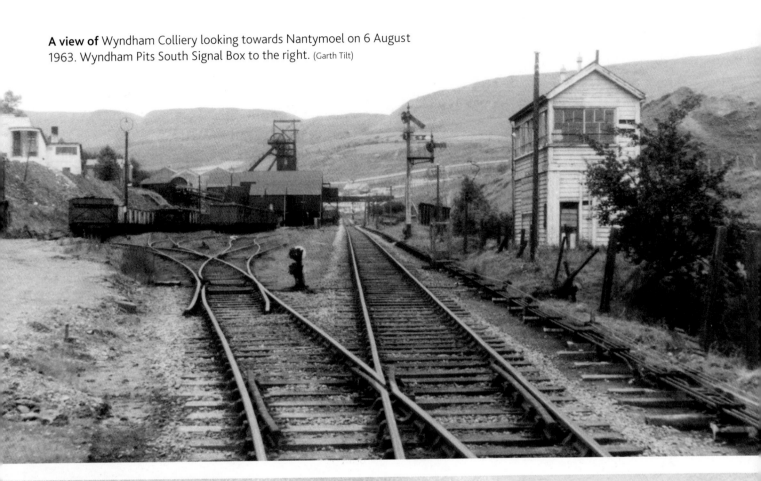

A view of Wyndham Colliery looking towards Nantymoel on 6 August 1963. Wyndham Pits South Signal Box to the right. (Garth Tilt)

A 1905 view at Wyndham with a rake of empty Cory Brothers Mineral Wagons. (D. Chandler collection/Kidderminster Railway Museum)

The screens at Wyndham Colliery in 1980 by when a fleet of vacuum-fitted 16tonners was available in South Wales as can be seen in the picture. Fitted wagons were unable to be used for shipment traffic as the vacuum pipes interfered with the equipment on the coal hoists but by 1980 little such traffic existed. The last train out of Wyndham Colliery ran on 21 October 1983.

Wyndham Colliery and Pit Head Baths, Ogmore Village

The extent of the Wyndham Colliery can be seen in this 1937 picture of the Cory Brothers Cardiff owned mine. The picture was taken to record the opening of the Pithead Baths seen on the left. Note the many 10ton wooden wagons, the standard form of transport for coal traffic at that time. All wagons then carried the name of the owner on the side and each had to be shunted out and returned to the owning colliery for re-loading until common ownership was introduced in 1942 by the Government to reduce the shunting workload to be encompassed in wartime, though it was a while before it was introduced in practice. Ownership then passed to the railway, producing increased costs of upkeep and provision. (Author's collection)

Collieries

Wyndham Colliery was sunk in 1865, a landmark year for pit development in the area, by the Llynvi, Tondu & Ogmore Vale Iron & Coal Co. The initial sinking of the two shafts was to the Six-Feet seam and was completed in 1868 but in 1891 they were deepened to just below the Bute seam at a depth of almost 1,077ft. Other seams worked at Wyndham at this time were the Gellideg with a thickness of 48ins, the Five-Feet with a combined thickness of 93ins, but with intermediate layers of dirt of 15ins, the Seven-Feet or Yard seam of 61ins., and the Bute, also known as the Yard, seam of up to 66ins. The Lower-Nine-Feet seam was also worked as the Yard seam and was 59ins thick, the Caerau or Red Vein seam was 71ins thick, the Lower-Six-Feet seam ranged from 66 to 84ins thick and was extensively worked, as was the Two-Feet-Nine seam which ranged from 60 to 68ins thick, though with an intermediate dirt band of 6 to 42ins, leading to the seam being split between top coal and bottom coal. Finally, the No. 3 Rhondda seam accessed by a Wyndham Level produced a thickness of coal of 28ins. Wyndham was indeed the most prolific of pits.

The original owning company went bankrupt in 1888 and was bought by a group under Colonel North for £350,000, to become part of North's Navigation Collieries (1899) Ltd. Output in 1889 was put at just shy of 180,000.tons and in 1899 manpower was 877. In 1906 Wyndham was sold to Cory Bros. and then employed 1,100-1,200 miners. This number gradually increased, normally totalling 1,300 to 1,500 through the 1920s and 30s, with a peak of just over 1,600 in 1920 itself.

In 1942, the colliery came under the control of the Powell Duffryn Steam Coal Co. Ltd., who in 1943 replaced steam with electricity as the main means of power. The number of staff employed at Wyndham, was by now down to less than a thousand at 950-970 with just over 900 at Nationalisation when production was 230,000 tons a year. Throughout the 1950s, production remained in the region of 200,000 with 850-900 employed.

Between 1957 and 1965, Wyndham was merged with neighbouring Western Colliery, at a cost of £3m and the estimated reserves of the combined position was 62m tons from the nine seams worked. The Wyndham downcast shaft was deepened by 120 yards to a depth of 435 yards and the Western upcast shaft to 476 yards. A roadway 315 yards in length was driven to connect the pits and was completed in 1962. New winders of 600 and 1700hp were installed at Western and Wyndham No. 1. Western's production was taken by underground conveyor to a bunker 1,300 yards from Wyndham pit bottom and taken from there to the Wyndham shaft by three diesel locos. The target production from the two pits was 15,000 tons per week, which the Wyndham shaft was easily capable of lifting. Cages were double deck and could wind 28 men or 3 tons of materials per lift, with all supplies for the complex handled via the Western shaft.

In 1971, the combined workforce of 1,188 men produced 475,000 tons, the highest output of a unit in the South Wales coalfield, from the Bute, Five-Feet and Gellideg seams. Towards the end of the 1970s, an area of 16 sq. miles of the Bute and Gellideg seams was being worked to a depth of 2,000 feet. Eight miles of underground roadways were involved with five miles of conveyors and one mile of loco haulage. Output per manshift at the two coalfaces in use was 4.5tonnes and overall for the colliery was 1.2tonnes. However, annual output for 1978 was just over half the tonnage for 1971 at 250,000 with just over 1,000 employed and in 1979 only 144,000 with just under 1,000 employed.

In a bid to improve production and working conditions, the NCB invested £1.7 million to open up a new area of the Five-Feet seam and in 1981 this seam was being worked at a thickness of some 60ins with a coalface length of between 400-600ft. Colliery output per day was targeted at 930tonnes, with Output per Man Shift (OMS) set at 4.91tonnes and overall for the colliery at 1.51tonnes. Saleable coal yield was however only 65 per cent of total production with the added cost of overland transport to Ogmore Vale Central Washery. Working conditions were however poor and better clothing protection from the cold was needed when working at such a depth. This and other problems being encountered led the NCB to bring an end to production because of the adverse mining conditions in 1984. By then, the workforce was down to 537 when the colliery was closed in 1984.

Western Colliery was sunk in 1873 by David Davies and associates, some 400 yards south-east of Nantymoel on the site of the original BlaenOgwr colliery. The down shaft was sunk to 318 yards deep, with the up to 380ft. and were 50 yards apart and cost almost £66,000 to sink, with production starting in 1876. The seams worked were the Two-Feet-Nine seam 60 ins thick at 257 yards deep, the Four-Feet at 277 yards, the Six-Feet at 318 yards, the Caerau or Red Vein 54ins thick at 320 Yards and the Nine-Feet at 349 yards. Also worked were the Middle Seven-Feet with a thickness of 42ins, the Bute seam (called here the Brunts seam) of 66ins, the Lower-Nine-Feet (also called the Bute) of 71ins, the Caerau or Red Vein of 54ins, and the Lower-Six-Feet of up to 84ins.

In 1887, Davies founded the Ocean Coal Company with capital increased to £800,000, secured by the issue of 8,000 shares of £100 each, of which almost half were held by Davies and his son Edward. The Head Office of the Company was at Bute Crescent, Cardiff Docks. Nine collieries were owned, employing almost 8,000 miners and producing a combined 2.75 million tons of coal. There were industrial interests and engineering projects in several countries, which combined to produce company assets of almost £5 million with annual profits of some £300,000. In 1889, the Western Colliery produced just over 250,000 tons of coal which by 1894 had risen to just under 300,000, the workforce up to 1920 normally being between 8-900. The late 1920s saw the figure rise to over 1,000 but during the 1930s it returned to its 1920s level.

At Nationalisation in 1947, Western Colliery employed 860 and output in 1948 was 210,000 with 850 employed, working on the Two-Feet Nine, Bute and Three-Feet-Ten seams. Output remained at between 200-250,000 tons during the 1950s with a workforce in the range 885 in 1950 falling to 697 in 1960. During this period, there was much concern at the high level of accidents at the colliery, from both National Union of Mineworkers (NUM) and NCB alike.

From 1965, Western Colliery was merged with nearby Wyndham and in 1971 the combined production was almost 475,000 tons, the highest for any production unit in the South Wales coalfield. Details of the workings of the combined unit are given under Wyndham Colliery. The combined unit was closed by the NCB in January 1984, the reason given being poor mining conditions.

A view of the Nantymoel station area in 1915 with a 1076 Class and three coaches of early bogie stock. Note the proximity of the residential area to the station, a feature of many valley towns.
(Lens of Sutton)

Fast forward to early Nationalisation days with this view of Tondu's 7770 with two non-corridor valley coaches on the 3.00pm to Bridgend on 28 September 1951. (W.A. Camwell/SLS)

A 1955 panoramic view of Nantymoel with the customary two coach formation here with both a conventional auto trailer and a conversion. The run-round loop had two lengths to cater for longer trains to be run round, used for the loco hauled specials that ran to Porthcawl at weekends but unnecessary on this occasion. (R.O. Tuck/Rail Archive Stephenson)

With the closure of some branch line services, serviceable stock was moved to other areas. The withdrawal of auto services between Pontypridd and Ynysybwl and Machen led to these two gas lit auto coaches W37 and W28 of diagrams N and A10 respectively being reallocated to Tondu on 16 September 1953 for the introduction of auto train operation a week later with five converted 55XX engines. Here we see 5560 with the 2.45pm Nantymoel to Bridgend on 14 August 1954. (N.L. Browne)

Another view of the same pair of auto coaches this time with 5545 on a service to Bridgend with Nantymoel SB visible five chains south of the platform. The box was closed in January 1964. The line from Ogmore Vale was at a steady rise of 1:41 while a gradient board at the end of the platform proclaimed a final flourish, for the last few yards of 1:27. (T.J. Edgington)

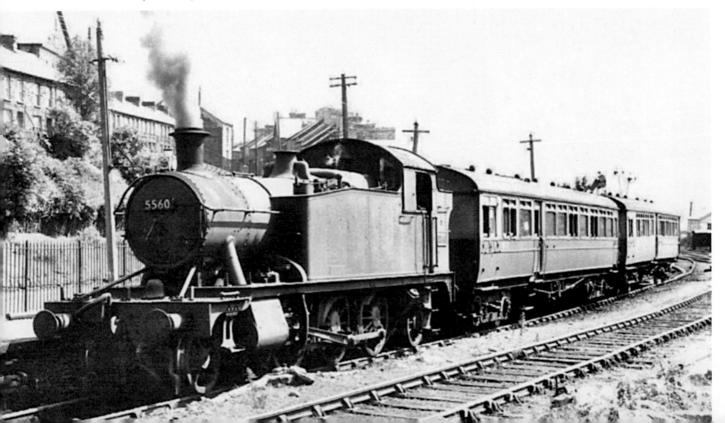

In addition to the purpose-built Auto Trailers, a number of non-corridor compartment coaches were converted for auto working on Valleys services and here 5545 arrives at Nantymoel with the 1.55pm from Bridgend seen from the north end of the platform on 11 April 1958.
(Robert Darlaston)

On the Christmas Eve 1957, 5545 stands in the headshunt in the process of running round her train of conventional stock. This truly is the limit of the branch.
(David Russell)

Topographically downhill all the way but being of GW pedigree, 'Up' to Bridgend. 5545 at Nantymoel ready for the 'off' on 24 December 1957. (David Russell)

The Stephenson Locomotive Society ran an enthusiasts' special to the Tondu Valleys on 2 July 1960, just over two years after Nantymoel station had been closed. Though the tracks are rusty, little appears to have changed to the infrastructure in those two years and even the T board remains.

6 August 1963 with a view of Nantymoel looking north. The run round loop has a temporary stop-block clearly an indication it is no longer in use.
(Garth Tilt)

On the same date another view looking down the valley and including the Signal Box which was closed on 3 January 1964. The station building seems to be self-demolishing.
(Garth Tilt)

CHAPTER 2

GARW BRANCH

BRYNMENYN

Covered in Chapter 1, Ogmore Branch

LLANGEINOR

The first location north of Brynmenyn on the Garw branch was Llangeinor, the station there being 2 miles from the junction. A quarter mile south of the station was the Bettws Llantwit Colliery with two loop sidings on the south side of the single line shown on a plan for 1876 before the station was built. A PSA for the colliery sidings was granted to William Boyle in July 1880 and in November 1891, the colliery was shown as owned by the Garw Llantwit Colliery Co. Ltd., before closing in 1904-6.

In 1890, the line was doubled between 1.51ch and 2m 6ch, to include the colliery sidings, outwards traffic controlled by Bettws Llantwit SB (closed in 1907) and the doubled platform station directly north of which was a LC controlled by Llangeinor SB. By 1915, the southern section of the double line had become an Up and Down Goods Loop (northern track) and a bi-directional single running line (southern track).

North of the station was the Llangeinor Colliery, accessed north of the double running line. Opened in 1908 with a PSA in February to the Llangeinor Colliery Co. Ltd., the colliery went into liquidation in 1911 and the access siding had been removed by May of that year.

After closure of the passenger service in 1953, the Up and Down Goods loop south of the station was taken out of use in June 1959 but was not recovered until February 1964. The line was singled above Llangeinor in October 1964.

A view along the platforms looking north on 13 July 1959. The station is now closed to passenger traffic but is still quite intact with the level crossing and signal box at the north end of the station. (R.M. Casserley)

A closer view of the level crossing, signal box and station building some eight years after withdrawal of the passenger service, with the surface having been taken off the platform on 13 June 1962.

14 October 1967 The Warwickshire Railway Society's Class 120 3 x Car Unit passes through on its return from Blaengarw.

D6930 heads towards Tondu with another load of
Garw Coal on 15 February 1973.

By the 1990s Llangeinor was just plain line with little
evidence of its busier past.

PONTYRHYLL

South End

Just over a mile further north from Llangeinor was Pontyrhyll where the Port Talbot Railway (PTR, opened in February 1898) met the Garw branch of the L&O, running parallel on the approach.

A drawing for 1890 shows the single line from Llangeinor becoming double south of Pontyrhyll station which was then still only composed of a northbound platform, with a SB, opened in 1886, south of the station on the south side of a loop siding serving a goods shed and yard, south of the running lines. On the north side of the line, a siding connection ran north to serve a large colliery complex at Braich-y-Cymmer.

By 1900, the Port Talbot Railway had joined the Garw branch from the south with a double line connection south of the station which had by now been provided with a southbound (up) platform, offset from the northbound (down) due to the colliery connection at 3¼ mp on the north side of the line.

In January 1949, the connecting lines with the former Port Talbot Railway were reduced to siding status. The PTR passenger service was withdrawn from 12 September 1932 and the Garw branch service from 9 February 1953. In September 1961, rationalisation of the area took place when Pontyrhyll SB was closed, sidings in the station goods yard removed and the former PTR sidings taken out of use. This left double lines running through to Pontycymmer, which were then singled in October 1964.

North End

To the north of Pontyrhyll was Braich-y-Cymmer where several collieries existed until the 1920s and 30s.

A plan for 1876 shows a long connection north of the single line and the Garw River serving Lluest Colliery, recorded as open by 1880, though the first PSA was February 1886 and closed in 1932. A plan for 1897 shows the Lluest Colliery complex as of a considerable size, the sidings at the north and south end and the screens covering about half a mile with tramroads along the north side. A PSA was granted in 1909 to the Llangeinor Colliery Co. Ltd. but in 1911, it was shown as in liquidation. Within the complex was the Duchy Colliery and that colliery company had a PSA for the North Jct. into the complex dated January 1915. It passed to the Lluest (or Llest) Collieries Ltd. in October 1925, before the colliery complex closed in April 1932, leaving a huge vacuum on the north side of the line.

South of the running line opposite the long inlet to the Lluest Colliery, the 1876 plan shows an inlet to the West Rhondda Colliery which must have been open by that time, though the first record of a PSA is for 1886. Though the PSA was shown as terminated in 1893 and the sidings removed, the site was apparently re-used with a PSA to Ambrose Emerson dated April 1895 before the connection with the running line is shown as removed in August 1911.

Further north, still on the south side of the line, the 1876 plan shows a Garw Colliery, with a PSA dated December 1881 to Messrs. Morgan. The 1897 plan shows this as the Garw Fechan Colliery with a tramway running south from the loading area alongside the running line. In June 1889, the PSA passed to Edwards & Emerson, suggesting that Emerson's involvement with the West Rhondda site was linked to the Garw Fechan. In October 1893, the PSA was in the name of Emerson only and in April 1897 to J. Emerson, then passing in March 1922 to the International Coal Co., before the colliery closed in April 1927.

North of the Garw Fechan Colliery, as the line swung west following the contour of the river, Braich-y-Cymmer Colliery was spread between the 3¾ and 4mps, with tramroads stretching out to the west alongside the running line. Though the colliery must have been open in 1876 to be on the plan of that date, the first PSA was dated December 1886 in the name of Edwards & Emerson (Braich-y-Cymmer Collieries). In October 1893, it stood in the name of Emerson only and was transferred to J. Emerson in April 1897. In March 1922, the colliery was sold to the International Coal Co. Ltd. and closed in April 1927.

The only SB along this mile of colliery dominated line, doubled in 1886, was at Braich-y-Cymmer on the north side of the line near the inlet to Duchy and Lluest Collieries. It was opened in 1886 and closed in 1933. The line was singled between Pontycymmer and Llangeinor in October 1964, by when all the above collieries had long since disappeared.

Due to the confined space, Pontyrhyll had staggered platforms. This view shows the northbound platform towards Blaengarw, seen from the north end of the southbound platform. The service was extended to Pontycymmer on 1 June 1889.
(Author's collection)

The station approach at Pontyrhyll.
(Author's collection)

East from Pontyrhyl Railway Station

A view of the railway running through Pontyrhyll probably from the late 1960s or 1970s after all sidings had been removed and the railway was double track.

A view looking south at Pontyrhyll dated 6 August 1963. It shows the former alignment of the Port Talbot Railway on the right heading for Llettybrongu, Maesteg (Neath Road), Bryn and ultimately the docks at Port Talbot. (Garth Tilt)

A view looking south on 6 August 1963 with the main station building on the Down platform still in place. (Garth Tilt)

Running north through Pontyrhyll on 29 February 1984 with a train of empty 21ton Minfits is Type 3 diesel 37271, shortly before the Miners' Strike which began on 12 March. The track had by now been singled. (Acton Wells Junction)

Between Pontyrhyll and Pontycymmer was Pantygog where we see 37905 running north with a train of 50ton coal empties to the Ffaldau tip clearance site on 27 April 1995. (S. Warr)

PONTYCYMMER

A plan for 1876 shows a single line running through Pontycymmer between the 4½ and 5mp from Brynmenyn Junction. A small passenger platform with a SB on the north end is shown with a Goods Siding north of the running line. By 1885, the Goods Siding had become the outlet from the nearby Ffaldau Colliery and two loop sidings had been built on the south side of the line, south of the platform, which may have been replacement public sidings for mileage and goods traffic. The station platform was extended and enlarged on plans for 1885/97 and 1914. A LC was shown at the north end of the platform on the plan for 1897 and the SB was renewed on the north side of the line in 1902, the new box lasting until May 1964 when replaced by a GF which itself only lasted until October 1964.

The line was doubled south of Pontycymmer in 1886 and through to Blaengarw in May 1902. The line was singled southwards between Pontycymmer and Llangeinor in October 1964 and north to Blaengarw in 1966.

North of the inlets to Ffaldau and Victoria Collieries was Victoria SB at the 5mp. Opened in 1902, it remained in service until May 1964 controlling the supply of empty wagons into both collieries.

The 1875 plan shows the projected layout for the Ffaldau Colliery north of the line around the 4¾mp. Opened in 1876 by the Ffaldau Steam Coal Co., it was also known as Oriental, producing both steam and house coal. Opposite Ffaldau Colliery on the south side of the line was Victoria Colliery, owned by the Ffaldau Steam Coal Co. Both collieries developed into larger undertakings as seen on the 1897 and 1914 plans of the area and by 1918, Ffaldau had been integrated with the Braich-y-Cymmer colliery. Production at Ffaldau was suspended in 1926 and it was kept as a pumping station only. However, it was soon back in production and in August 1934, the whole undertaking passed into the hands of Cory Bros. of Cardiff, who later sold it on to Powell Duffryn, until nationalisation in 1947. It was a prolific pit and after nationalisation underwent a major reconstruction.

The NCB merged the colliery with the neighbouring Garw (Ocean) Colliery in April 1975, Ffaldau finally closing in December 1985. The branch remained in existence as far as Pontycymmer until 1986, purely to serve Ffaldau Colliery. The branch was in use until 1995 for reclaimed spoil, from which date the Bridgend Valleys Railway was instigated with a plan to operate the branch to Tondu as a heritage railway.

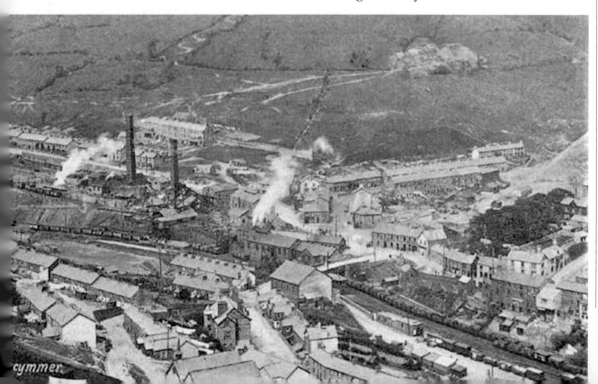

A panoramic view of Ffaldau Colliery dated to 1906 with the staggered Up platform to Blaengarw visible and the approach roads to the station clearly shown. (Author's collection)

A view of a passenger train leaving Pontycymmer station for Blaengarw, formed of three bogie coaches which might date the photograph to c1900. (Author's collection)

Seen from the brakevan of a train of loaded coal from Blaengarw, a full view of the staggered up platform at Pontycymmer, located south of the road bridge on 13 July 1959. (H.C. Casserley.)

A plan for 1890 shows that between the 5 and 5½mp, just north of Pontycymmer, were connections with the Darren Fawr or Victoria Colliery which was opened in April 1883 by James & Co., as part of the Braich-y-Cymmer complex. It employed 217 men in 1903, 168 in 1905 and 246 in 1909. It was owned by the Garw & Braich-y-Cymmer Collieries Co. and closed in 1921.

With the photographer riding in the brakevan of a train of empties heading for Blaengarw, this view is of a section of Pontycymmer station's up staggered platform as the train approaches the signal box and road bridge on 13 July 1959. (R.M. Casserley)

A view along the up staggered platform at Pontycymmer with loaded wagons in a down siding as Tondu's 4241 takes water at the water column at the south end of the down platform in the distance on 13 July 1959. (H.C. Casserley)

The staggered down platform at Pontycymmer seen from the road bridge on 13 July 1959 with wagons of washed small coal for SCOW Margam and wagons of sized coal in the sidings awaiting despatch. (R.M. Casserley)

Viewed from the road bridge which separated the up and down platforms, Tondu's 4241 taken water from the water column on the south end of the platform with turn U18, a block train of washed small coking coal from Blaengarw to SCOW Margam, running as Class 9 on 13 July 1959. (R.M. Casserley)

A view of Pontycymmer looking towards Blaengarw dated 6 August 1963. The confined space of the valley floor is evident and explains why the station here had staggered platforms. (Garth Tilt)

Ffaldau Colliery looking south in 1986 with the railway checker's cabin in foreground and weighbridge in the distance.

Faldau Colliery during demolition in 1986.

A view looking north at Ffaldau Colliery sometime c1930.

Heading north towards Pontycymmer in March 1992, a Class 37 with an enthusiast special.

Reclaimed coal from International Colliery Tip was processed and worked through a new loading pad constructed at Pontycymmer in 1991-97 (with a run-round loop installed) 37905 arrives in the loop at Pontycymmer on 27 April 1995, where it will run round and then propel its train of empty wagons adjacent to the loading pad. This train then went forward loaded to Steel Supply, Briton Ferry. (S. Warr)

37801 appropriately named Aberddawan/Aberthaw whose Power Station was the destination of so much coal from the Tondu Valleys in the final years, is recorded loading spoil at Pontycymmer destined for Briton Ferry on 17 October 1992. (S. Warr)

37899 stands at the loading plant whilst a mechanical digger loads reclaimed spoil 'Duff' for Jersey Marine 3 October 1992. (S. Warr)

BLAENGARW

Railway

A plan of the area for 1877 shows a single line railway running to the end of the branch alongside the Garw River at 5m 74ch from Brynmenyn. Within the next 6 years, new mines at Garw, Pwllcarn and International would be sunk at the top of the Valley so that by the time the GWR produced a new plan of the area for 1890, its industrial nature was more clearly defined.

With the start of the passenger service in September 1902, the branch was re-aligned in May 1902 to run in a slightly more northerly position, perhaps due to the original alignment being very close to the river, and the line was doubled south to Pontycymmer. A new single platform was built for Blaengarw, separate from the running line leading to the collieries. Sidings serving Garw and International collieries were kept separate, the former on the east side of the running line, with those for the latter on the west side between the

37701 stands at the loading point with 7B65 1315 Pontycymmer-Briton Ferry Steel Supply on 7 March 1995. (S. Warr)

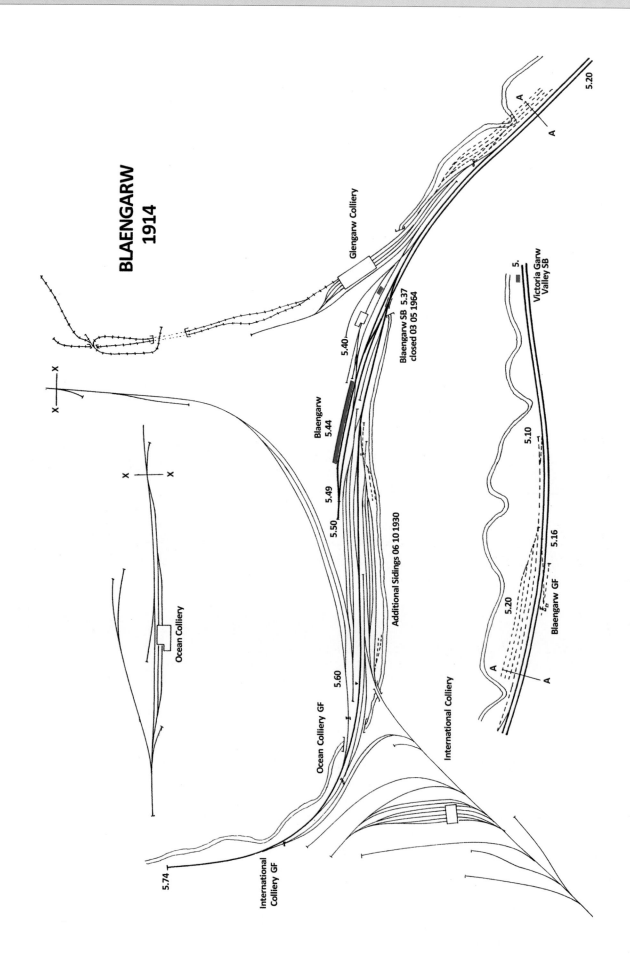

BLAENGARW 1914

Glengarw Colliery

Ocean Colliery

Ocean Colliery GF

International Colliery GF

5.74

International Colliery

Blaengarw SB 5.37
closed 03 05 1964

Additional Sidings 06 10 1930

Blaengarw
5.44

5.40

5.49

5.50

5.60

Victoria Garw
Valley SB

Blaengarw GF

5.20

5.10

5.16

5.20

5.

running line and the river. In July 1948, the freight lines north of the SB which was south of the passenger station, from 5m 38ch to the stop block at the end of the branch as 5m 74ch were sold to the NCB. Following the closure of the passenger service in 1953, the layout remained the same with coal traffic now using the previous passenger lines. Rationalisation in 1964 saw the running line cut back to 5m 16ch with all other lines to the north being taken over by the NCB. By 1981, the NCB had developed the layout into two nests of two and four loop sidings with a bunker for operation of Merry-Go-Round (MGR) services to Port Talbot Steelworks.

Garw Central Washery was set up to deal with all the coals produced in the Garw Valley and continued in production until December 1985 when the last coal was lifted at the Ocean/Ffaldau colliery. However, for a while, Garw coal passed to Ogmore Vale Central Washery to become part of the blend for Port Talbot Steelworks. The cost of rail conveyance badly affected the viability of the traffic and it was curtailed. The branch was then closed but re-opened in April 1986 to clear stock coal, the last train of which ran in May 1986. The branch continued in operation however to clear reclaimed coal from Pontycymmer Tip until 1997.

The single platform for passenger traffic was located at 5m.44ch., north-west of Glengarw Colliery on the east side of the running line, which was a loop to facilitate running round and ran on to another stop block at 5m.50ch., the mineral line having diverted at Blaengarw SB at 5m.37ch. to run on to serve the Garw and International Collieries. The SB was opened in April 1902 and closed in May 1964.

The branch remains extant but out of use pending development as a heritage railway.

Collieries

Blaengarw was a prolific coal mining area. The branch ended at 5m.74ch. from Brynmenyn Jct. In the 1880s, proceeding north from Pontycymmer, at the 5½mp were tramroads of the Nanthir or Glengarw Colliery which ran from the high ground on the east side of the line to loading points in sidings alongside the running line. At the top of the Valley were two major collieries, Garw (or Ocean) and International, both opened in 1883, with Pwllcarn Colliery between them which was soon merged with International.

Approaching Blaengarw from Pontycymmer, **Glengarw Colliery** (also known as Nanthir at opening, Victoria from 1889 and then Glengarw from 1907) was to be found on the east (up) side of the line, opening in 1875 and consisting of a slant with a tramway from higher ground bringing traffic down to two loading points alongside the running line. It was initially owned by the Nanthir Colliery Co. but in August 1900 was acquired by the New Blaengarw Colliery Co. and in November 1907 by the Glenavon & Garw Collieries Ltd. This company developed the undertaking from 1903 so that a plan for 1914 showed it as a fully-fledged colliery unit with screens, inward and outward sidings, the latter extended southwards by 1917. New PSAs were taken out with the GWR in 1910/13/17 to provide for extensions made. The Victoria and Yard seams were accessed in 1908, the Caedefaid drift was added in 1910, an upcast pit in 1912, and No. 3 pit opened in 1913. It also worked the Caedavid seam extensively, this seam formed by the merging of the Gorllwyn Rider and Gorllwyn seams in this area. The Upper Yard (or Centre) seam was also worked, while the Pentre Rider seam (also called the Victoria seam) was also worked extensively. To locals, Glengarw was also known as Ballarat, New Blaengarw, Blaengarw Victoria at different times.

The colliery produced both house and steam coals. In 1908 Glengarw employed 184 men underground and 12 on the surface, this expanding to a total of 540 men underground and 78 on the surface in 1913, 453/87 in 1918. No. 3 Slant was completed in 1924. In 1934, the total employed at this slant and the pit was 562/100. In March 1945, the company was taken over by Ocean Coal & Wilsons Ltd., who employed 366/69 men working the Victoria, Yard and Caedefaid seams. At Nationalisation in 1947, the figures were 365/71, working the same seams. The Caedefaid seam was abandoned in August 1951 and the Upper Yard in March 1952, so that by 1955 the number working at the coalface was down to 142 and 120 in 1958. Glengarw was closed by the NCB in November 1959, the Victoria (or Pentre Rider) seam having been abandoned as being uneconomic to work.

Garw (or Ocean) Colliery was located some quarter of a mile north-west of Glengarw, past where the passenger station would be located in 1902 for the start of the service from Bridgend. The colliery was opened by the Ocean Coal Company, founded by David Davies, of Barry Dock fame, in 1883 at a cost just shy of £47,000. The upcast and downcast ventilation shafts were 144ft apart and were sunk in 1884/5. The first coal was wound in 1886, with a subsidiary company – the Blaengarw Ocean Coal Company – formed to run the pit. In 1896, the pit employed 462 men underground and 78 on the surface. The Garw colliery was in a most prolific area with up to 20 seams available with a thickness from 32 to 72ins. This produced Types 203 and 204 Coking Steam Coal, with weak to medium and medium to strong caking, low volatile, low ash and sulphur content. This gave a wide variety of uses from steam raising in ships' boilers, locomotives and power stations, to foundry and blast furnace coke and coking blends. Initial annual production was between 150-200,000 tons, the normal annual output of all the collieries owned by the Ocean Company being some 2.5 million tons. Manpower at the colliery varied mostly between 500 and 800 but reached 931 in 1928/9.

In 1937, the Ocean Company purchased the nearby International Colliery and linked the two collieries as one production unit. The Ocean Company then merged with the owners of International, the United National Co., to become the Ocean & United National Collieries Ltd.

Published manpower figures for the two collieries were however kept separate. Prior to Nationalisation, in 1943/5 Garw employed 567 men underground and 115 on the surface and were working the Two-Feet-Nine and Three-Feet seams. Following Nationalisation, the colliery was equipped with its own Washery; production was at first 150,000 tons p.a., rose to 190,000 in 1954 but then settled at 160-170,000 to 1961 with a workforce of between 6-700.

In 1975, Garw was merged with Ffaldau at a cost of £86,000, with all coal being brought up at Garw. 3.2tons of coal could be raised per wind or 28 men. Eleven miles of underground roadways were in use with four miles of conveyors. At the time of merger, an estimated 7.5 million tons of reserves was quoted between the two pits. The new boundaries of the underground take were given as the Glyncorrwg geological fault to the east and the Blaengarw fault to the west. Average OMS at the coalface was 4.4tonnes and overall for the colliery 1.5tonnes. Average saleable output was 5,300 tonnes per week, equivalent to two trainloads per day. Saleable coal yield was 60 per cent. The first year of the merger saw production at 367,000 tonnes but this declined gradually through the 1970s and by 1982 it was down to 139,000 tons, the workforce having fallen from 902 in 1978 to 730 in 1982. Following the miners' strike of 1984/5, production recovered to 89 per cent of the norm but adverse geological conditions were met in some areas which had to be closed down, resulting in a production level of 7,500 tonnes per week being necessary to keep the pit viable. This was unattainable, and the combined unit was closed in December 1985 as being uneconomic.

Slightly further along the branch on the west side, the 1877 plan shows Pwllcarn Colliery. This colliery opened in 1874 by John Thomas, and was operated by a partnership of seven people as 'Thomas, Sons & Davies' and subsequently as the Pwllcarn Colliery Co. In May 1883, the Transatlantic Steam Coal Co. was formed to acquire Pwllcarn Colliery and the company began sinking their own pits. The company ceased trading in 1885 and in June 1886 the International Steam Coal Co. Ltd. took it over, and in later developments it became part of the International colliery.

International Colliery, on the western side of the head of the Garw Valley, was also opened in 1883, a short distance from Garw. As such it accessed much the same seams as Garw of between 25 and 72ins thickness. The colliery was nicknamed the 'Carn' and comprised three shafts, the first two sunk in 1883, the No. 1 Pit downcast to a depth of 309 yards, later deepened to 479 yards, and the No. 2 Pit upcast to 390 yards, just below the Bute seam. The No. 3 pit shaft was sunk in 1910, to the Caedavid seam at 123 yards. The mineral take of International was squeezed between North's Navigation Collieries to the west and south, Oriental to the southeast and Ocean to the east and north. It was sunk by John Davies & Co. (possibly the Transatlantic Steel & Coal Co.) who owned the small nearby Pwllcarn colliery, but it was sold on to the International Coal Co. Ltd. in April 1889 which had a capital of £85,000. The colliery was highly successful and by 1889 employed 916 men.

The decision to sink No. 3 Pit in 1910 resulted from the strong demand for South Wales coal across the world and by 1913, International employed 1013 men. In 1915 the owning company had assets of over £108,000 and a share value of £85,000. Profits had been £40,000 in 1900 and £30,000 in 1901 but this dropped significantly year on year with good results in 1907/8, but generally producing less than £12,000. In 1928, the International Co. came into the hands of its neighbour the Glenavon Garw Colliers Ltd., which by 1935 controlled six pits employing 3,340 men and producing 850,000 tons per annum, the International portion of this being 800 men underground and 67 on the surface. This ownership was short-lived as it soon passed into the hands of Guest Keen & Nettlefold but again only for about six weeks before ending with the Ocean Coal Company

who formed a subsidiary company, the International Colliery Company (Blaengarw) Ltd., which ran the colliery until Nationalisation in 1947.

The late 1920s and 30s were a very difficult time for the collieries and people of the Garw Valley due to the number of temporary mine closures and part time working, much of which was down to dissension caused by non-unionism in the area, with International having 600 miners who were not members of the South Wales Miners Federation. Periods of strikes, including stay-downs, lock outs and civil unrest from 1929-35 were eventually followed by a victory for the union and anti-unionism in the area collapsed.

At Nationalisation, the colliery employed 415 underground and 115 on the surface and was working the Nine-Feet and No. 6 seams. In 1949, the NCB announced that the colliery was closing and 150 miners were transferred to neighbouring pits but the decision was reversed. By 1954, the same seams were being worked as in 1947 but now with only 211 men underground and 78 on the surface. The aborted closure decision had far-reaching implications in the relations between colliery management and the workforce resulting in a joint NCB/NUM inquiry into the pit ten years later with allegations of indifference towards repairs necessary and confrontations on wages, even though International was one of the top four pits for OMS in South Wales. This was only solved when the NCB retired the manager, but production remained low and though it had been 120,000 tons in 1948/9, it had fallen to 106,000 in 1955 and decreased year on year to only 57,000 in 1961 by when the workforce had fallen to about 300. The NCB finally closed the colliery in November 1967.

Coal produced at International was classed as Type 203 and 204 Coking Steam Coal, the 203 being low to medium caking and the 204 medium to strong caking. These coals were used for steam raising, for foundry and blast furnace coke and for coking blends. Ash content was around 5 per cent.

A c1903 view from a southerly aspect, south of the footbridge which spanned the tracks south of the station and goods complex. This view shows the railway layout serving the collieries, station and goods shed and shows a three-coach train of possibly six wheelers. Little access to Ocean or International Collieries north of the station is seen while south of the layout shown is the line to Glengarw Colliery which went off to the left of the bottom row of houses. The Blaengarw Hotel is seen above the goods shed and there is the usual supply of chapels to keep the residents on the straight and narrow. (Author's collection)

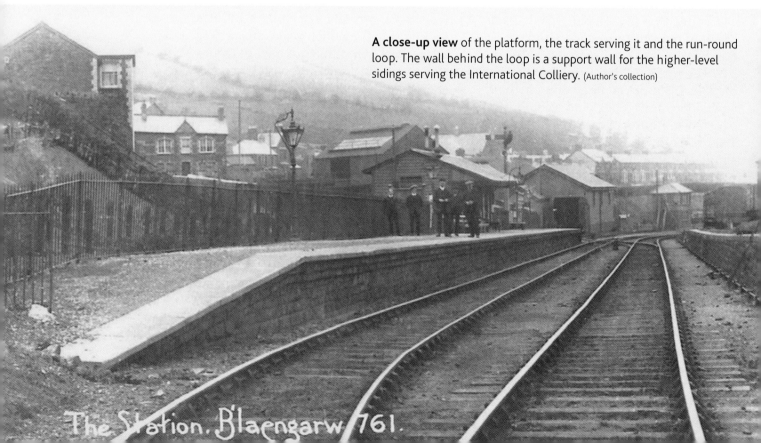

A close-up view of the platform, the track serving it and the run-round loop. The wall behind the loop is a support wall for the higher-level sidings serving the International Colliery. (Author's collection)

The Station. Blaengarw 761.

To prove that the sun does shine in the Welsh Valleys, this lovely view of the 4pm from Brynmenyn running into Blaengarw on 28 September 1951 with Tondu's 5797 in charge. The signal box can be seen in the right distance and the goods shed a little further north. (Gerald T. Robinson)

Standing at the single platform on 2 August 1951, with a two-coach train to Brynmenyn where it will join up with a similar train from Nantymoel, Tondu's 9660 prepares to depart. Note the gate which is a vestige of the past when access was gated off at the bottom of the station slope when a train was ready to depart. (R.C. Riley/Transport Treasury)

A two coach service to Brynmenyn and Bridgend awaits the signal for departure in 1951 behind a Tondu pannier with the extent of the run-round loop clearly visible, leading also into the goods yard. On the left the sidings serving International Colliery can be seen with one of its two shafts while sidings serving Ocean Colliery can be seen at a higher level in the centre background. (Ian Wright)

The 3.10pm service on 13 September 1952 behind Tondu's 3668. Ocean Colliery sidings can be seen on the left middle of the view with part of the station building visible on the platform. (W. Potter/KRM)

In the Washery sidings at the north end of the Blaengarw colliery complex, Tondu's 4241 will collect a train of coking coal probably for the Steel Co. of Wales at Margam on 13 July 1959. (H.C. Casserley)

During the 1960s and 70s, there were several enthusiasts' specials run by railway societies which included the Tondu Valleys and these often provide some interesting views of layouts as here when SLS Special 2Z37 with engine 6416 included a tour of the Garw Branch on 2 July 1960 in its itinerary of the Tondu and Swansea Valleys. This view is from north of the station showing the train at the platform and empty minerals for supply to the International or Ocean Colliery at a slightly higher level on the right with the extremity of the running line in the foreground, the remaining tracks being NCB. (Hugh Davies Collection)

After the long climb from Tondu, locally based 4251 arrives at Blaengarw on 1 June 1962 with a train of empty minerals from Margam, showing the layout at the south end of the complex under the control of the signal box on the extreme left.
(B.W.L. Brooksbank/Initial Photographics)

Blaengarw viewed on 6 August 1963 looking towards the head of the valley with much of the original infrastructure still intact including the station and goods shed (extreme right). (Garth Tilt)

A view looking south along the Platform at Blaengarw on 6 August 1963. (Garth Tilt)

Another view taken on 6 August 1963 with a close-up of the station building looking rather forlorn. Passenger services were withdrawn in 1953 but the running-in board remains as does the Starter Signal. (Garth Tilt)

A view looking towards the station on 4 August 1964. The SB was closed on 3 May and is here in the throes of demolition. (Garth Tilt)

This view of Blaengarw, taken on 20 June 1970, shows how the Passenger and Goods facilities have been removed and the only revenue earner is coal. (Garth Tilt)

Tip clearance in progress in July 1972, alongside where Blaengarw station platform used to exist. All sidings in the area are now taken over by the NCB and a train of EMWs is standing alongside the reclaimed duff being loaded by grab. The bank behind may have been the source of the reclaimed coal from its appearance.

37 184 working 9B94 returns an NCB Austerity Tank after repair at Cardiff Canton depot on 11 February 1975. (S. Warr)

At the end of the line at Ocean Colliery on 29 February 1984, Type 3 37271 waits to reverse a train of empty 21ton Minfits under the screens for loading to Margam Steelworks. The colliery closed in December 1985.

TIP RECLAMATION

The line reopened to Pontycymmer in 1991 when a new loading pad and run round loop were installed in order to remove coal reclaimed from colliery tips at the site of the former International Colliery. The end of the line was now south of Garreg crossing at 5m 16ch. The first loaded train on 26 November 1991 ran to Steel Supply Briton Ferry with coal for blending but the destination changed to Aberthaw Power station on 6th March 1996. The last train to Aberthaw ran on 6 March 1997 and was the last coal train out of the Tondu valleys.

On 23 October 1996, Mike Back recorded a complete working of one of these in the Garw Valley first as an empty MGR train, running as 6Z30 and hauled by 37412 from Tondu to the loading point at Pontycymmer, and then returning loaded down the Valley as far as Tondu. The following twelve images show the empty train passing Brynmenyn and Tylagwyn, between Pontyrhyll and Pontycymmer, before arriving at Pontycymmer where the train was loaded from the stock of reclaimed coal. The train is then recorded running loaded as 7Z30 returning to Tondu and on to Aberthaw.

On 23 October 1996, this MGR service for Aberthaw was recorded in the Garw Valley by Mike Back. Running empty from Aberthaw, the MGR train 6Z30 with engine 37412 passes through the new station at Tondu before taking the junction for the Garw Branch.

Traversing the level crossing and bridge at the north end of the former Brynmenyn platform.

Heading north through Tylagwyn between Pontyrhyll and Pontycymmer on the single line seen from an overbridge off the main road up the Valley.

A panoramic view down the Valley from the main road shows the train negotiating the many curves as it makes its way up the Valley.

Approaching Pontycymmer as the train threads its way between the hills.

Passing the site of Pontycymmer station where a loop exists to enable engines to run round their train.

The engine has run round its train and draws wagons forward for loading by grab from the stock of reclaimed coal on the ground.

Another view of the train being loaded at the stock site.

The train heads away from Pontycymmer on the double track section alongside the run-round loop with its well loaded wagons for Aberthaw running as 7Z30.

Descending the Garw Valley through Tylagwyn, the train negotiates the single line.

The loaded train approaches Brynmenyn. The Travelling shunter with Train Staff in hand is about to open the level crossing.

The train pauses alongside Tondu Signal Box and the Driver surrenders the Token for the Garw Branch before taking the line to Bridgend where it will access the Vale of Glamorgan line for Aberthaw Power Station.

CHAPTER 3

PORTHCAWL BRANCH

TONDU

The Porthcawl branch was the southwestern fork of the four-way junction at Tondu, the station platforms consisting of a single Up platform from Porthcawl and a Down platform which was part of the triangular platform layout with the Llynfi & Ogmore section. Unlike the L&O where Down trains ran north into Tondu, with the Porthcawl services, it was the Up trains.

A plan for 1875 shows sidings on both sides of the running lines which were double from an early date, with two long loop sidings on the west side running through to Tondu North with three shorter sidings on the east side, running down to Velin Vach SB (an anglicised version of Welsh Felin Fach) which controlled all movements southwards on the Porthcawl side of the station. A LC was situated just north of the point where the line became double for station access with the original Velin Vach SB on its south side. This closed in 1886 and was replaced by a new box north of the LC, the new box itself closing in 1895. West of the station was the huge Tondu Ironworks, opened in 1838 by Sir Robert Price, covering a very considerable area and made up of a Gas Works, Brick Works and Engine Shed at the north end of the complex. The Ironworks itself was in the centre of the complex with Coke Ovens to the south, and long sidings stretching east under the Porthcawl branch line, to Brogdens SB on the Tondu to Bridgend branch and to Park Slip Colliery to the south.

A plan for 1897 shows that the area between the Porthcawl and the Bridgend branches at Tondu was soon to be taken over by North's Navigation Colliery which opened there in 1906 and would quickly develop into a large scale colliery with Washery and Coke Ovens with the long siding to Park Slip still in being. North's owned the Iron Works, the coal from this colliery being used to supply that works. There had been a previous colliery on the site which had closed before the plan for 1875 was produced. It is only referred to as the 'Old Colliery' with no further details.

The Down Porthcawl Platform at Tondu station had now become an island with a bay on the inside of the fork and five long sidings for stabling alongside feeding into a long siding stretching down beyond Velin Vach box. South of the box, Evanstown Brickworks opened in 1911 on the west side of the line. Owned initially by W. Johnson, it was taken over by Tondu Brickworks Co. in 1933 and remained in business until the end of 1964 under the ownership of Star, Brick & Tile. It was accessed by Velin Vach GF which lasted until January 1965.

Tondu Ironworks closed in 1878, though North's Navigation Colliery, the attached Washery and Coke Ovens, still occupied the site between the Bridgend and Porthcawl branches on a plan for 1940, with further coke ovens south of the wagon works. The long line from North's to these coke ovens, which had previously run all the way to Park Slip colliery had now been cut short at the coke ovens.

Velin Vach SB closed in June 1963 and was replaced by the Tondu Branch GF. The long headshunt on the down side running past Velin Vach SB lasted some time after the box closed and housed the South End Pilot (normally No. 4222) in the weeks before Tondu was dieselised.

A plan for 1967 shows no rail connection into any of the previous industrial concerns west of the station, though the

This view on
Saturday 5 September 1957 shows a 5 coach train waiting to depart from the Porthcawl Bay, the load increased from the normal weekday level. Note the amount of spare stock and loaded minerals for the weekend. The station nameboard clearly shows that passengers on this Porthcawl section of the station should change for the Llynvi and Ogmore services.
(M. Hale/GW Trust)

Wagon Works was not demolished until February 1989. The sidings alongside the Porthcawl platform were taken out of use in August 1970, following which only the Up and Down branch lines remained through the disused platform, becoming a single line south-westwards from a point 25 chains from the main junction.

Between half and three quarters of a mile south of Tondu, a plan for 1875 shows Cribbwr Colliery with Coke Ovens, located on the west side of the single line and accessed via Cribbwr GF at 0m.53ch. A PSA is shown to R. Evans, in being at the end of 1897 but believed to have been taken out much earlier. This passed to R.C. Griffiths in November 1907 and to W. Johnson in May 1910. A plan for 1915 shows the siding now leading to Cribbwr Brickworks and Coke Ovens, with a note of probable closure in 1923/4.

On the opposite side of the line, Aberkenfig Brickworks PS is shown as opening in 1913, owned by R. Jenkins with W. Johnson taking over in 1917. The works closed at the end of 1935.

Just west of the connection into Cribbwr Colliery, an 1897 plan shows Tondu and Cribbwr Ballast Sidings with two long loops running parallel with the single running line for Tondu and a siding off the connection into the colliery for the Cribbwr. Two tip sidings came off the North's Navigation line from their colliery in Tondu to Park Slip; these were gone on a 1915 plan but were shown again on a 1940 plan with the Ballast Sidings now reversed, so that the Cribbwr was now a loop siding where the former colliery connection had been. Both were taken out of use in 1965/6 as was the connection into the Tondu Brickworks in January 1965.

Just south of the Tondu Ballast Siding a plan for c1900 shows the Fountain Level Crossing, operated by a GF which was taken out of use at the end of 1967 when Automatic Half Barriers were provided. The road over the crossing was closed at the end of 1971 and the barriers removed.

The Porthcawl platform on 25 August 1962. Rationalisation has already started with the northbound arrival platform having already been taken out of service and partially recovered, all activities now being centred on the down platform. The locomotive shed can be seen in the Junction fork, the Llynvi branch to the left, Ogmore and Garw branches to the right. Trailing in from the right are the Up and Down lines to/from Bridgend, all this controlled from Tondu Middle Signal Box seen under the footbridge. From the Signal box, it was possible to see five others: Tondu North on the Llynvi Branch, Tondu Ogmore Junction on the Ogmore/Garw branch, Tondu South on the Bridgend Line, Velin Vach on the Porthcawl Branch, and finally Brynmenyn Junction where the Ogmore and Garw branches diverged. (Bluebell Archive)

May 1949 and small prairie 4404 at 1.35pm is ready to start the afternoon Porthcawl working from the Down (northbound) branch platform. Arriving with the 12.40pm from Porthcawl a 25-minute turn round enabled a crew change with locomotive coaling and servicing at the depot. The two-coach set in the down bay would form another service on the Porthcawl line. (Lens of Sutton)

Small Prairie 4557 with a service from Porthcawl in April 1952. The following year Auto trains were introduced with the larger capacity tanks of the 4575 sub-class (1300 gallons as opposed to 1000 gallons of the 45XX). 15 were adapted for this purpose of which 5 came to Tondu and ended the long presence of the small Prairies. (Ian L. Wright)

With a train of 4 carriages on 20 June 1953 it is undoubtedly a Saturday. 3627 has just arrived at Tondu with a service from Porthcawl on the last leg of the morning turn on the branch. There being no locomotive servicing facilities at Porthcawl, it was necessary to re-provision the locomotive at Tondu and as a result each timetable consisted of a service from Porthcawl around 12.30pm with a balancing return service from Tondu around 1.45pm. In theory, this could be achieved with the same resources but meant the train, if an Auto formation, all had to visit the coaling stage a rather cumbersome operation. In practice the two turns were performed using separate resources. (F.K. Davies)

6435 waits to depart from Tondu with the 1.40pm to Porthcawl at the start of the afternoon turn 21 August 1962. By this time the Up Porthcawl Branch Platform as can be seen was out of use. 6435 had been a long term Abercynon engine before being transferred to Tondu and worked the famous JB turn up and down the Barry Main Line between Pontypridd and Cardiff Clarence Road, as well as auto services to Ynysybwl and Machen. (Gerald T. Robinson)

6419 gets ready for the off with the 1.40pm to Porthcawl at the start of its afternoon turn on a sunny 5 September 1962. Spare passenger stock is held in the sidings on the left. (W.A. Brown)

At the end of the day (18 June 1962) 6431 propels the 7.25pm Auto from Porthcawl into the Bay platform at Tondu. The train is working under the control of hand signals since the bay at this time was under the control of the Velin Vach Yard Staff. The leading Trailer is W256 followed by W245. (Garth Tilt)

4222, Tondu's favourite 'Big Boy', works bunker first with house coal from Maesteg Central Washery for Margam Yard on 7 March 1964, five weeks before steam came to an end at Tondu. In good order, 4222 was transferred to Llantrisant but ended her days in the October. (S V Blencowe)

27 April 1995.
37905 with 6B73 0850 Jersey Marine to Pontycymmer empties en route to Pontycymmer tip, approaching the site of the former Porthcawl branch platforms. (D. Gatehouse)

A Class 37 heads a train of empties for Maesteg sometime in 1993. (D. Gatehouse)

Even in 1974, Tondu could still witness some intensive activity and here two Class 37s pass with loaded and empty mineral wagons to/from Margam steelworks, whilst another train of loaded awaits despatch. (S. Warr)

PARK SLIP COLLIERY

Park Slip Colliery was at the extreme southern outcrop of the South Wales Coalfield and at the end of the long internal line from North's Navigation Colliery at Tondu. The connection, sidings and screens were north of the single line at 1¼ miles from Tondu. The colliery, producing house and gas coal, was opened c1864 by John Brogden & Sons, who in 1872 merged with the Llynfi, Tondu & Ogmore Coal & Iron Co. but the venture failed in 1878 and it was eventually taken over by North's Navigation. A plan for 1875 shows three loop sidings under the screens with further sidings at the west

end, with the long siding from North's at Tondu joining at the east end. Access was controlled by GFs at both ends of the complex, named North and South, taken out of use in May 1967 following the colliery closure. The colliery lay idle from 1892-5 following an explosion due to an accumulation of gas which killed 110 men and boys. It re-opened in 1896 with some 270 men employed, closing again in 1904.

In 1918, North's purchased 3,000 acres of land around the colliery intending to sink three new pits and re-open the original which was now flooded. The colliery was re-opened in 1924 but only on a limited scale and it seems to have closed again later in that decade. In later years, it has become an opencast site and is still in being today, with the Tondu to Margam route remaining open for potential use from the site.

On the south side of the line approaching Park Slip Colliery was the Bridgend Dinas Brickworks. Opened during 1875 by the Cardiff Silica Firebrick Co., it passed in January 1883 to the New Bridgend Dinas Firebrick Co. and in June 1900 to P.L. Noel Fountain Works Co. The works closed in 1910 and the sidings were removed in 1911, access being from Park Slip North GF, open until 1967.

CEFN JUNCTION

Cefn Junction assumed that status when the Port Talbot Railway (PTR) opened on 19 December 1898 with its branch from Cefn into Port Talbot Docks. A plan for c1876 shows Ffos (or Ffoes) Pit on the south side of the single line approaching Cefn. In 1876, it was owned and managed by a William Williams but nothing more is known for certain about the pit which was not shown on the plan for 1899.

To the north of the single line (and the planned route from Cefn Jct. for the PTR) lay the Cefn Ironworks, Coke Ovens and Colliery. The Birmingham industrialist John Bedford built a blast furnace here in 1780 and sank mines to access the ironstone and coal deposits running along the southern fringe of the coalfield. He also founded a forge and brickworks. The ironworks were never as successful as hoped and declined after Bedford's death in 1791. The coal mining and brickworks continued through the nineteenth century but closed in 1904. The works then became the Pyle & Blaina Ferro Manganese Works which lasted until 1918.

A plan for 1899 shows a much-changed situation in the area. The line from Tondu was doubled approaching the new

Cefn Junction, here seen on 4 June 1965, was the start of the Ogmore Vale Extension Line from the Tondu Valleys into Margam, built by the Port Talbot Railway and opened on 19 December 1898. The line ran from Cefn Junction past Waterhall Sidings and Newlands to join the SWML at Margam Moors. The view shows the full double line junction, made by the existence of a passing loop on the branch. In September 1965 the branch to Margam was singled and in August 1966 the junction was moved east by a chain. With the closure of the line to Porthcawl on 19 November 1973, the branch became the main route and still survives for any traffic from the Tondu Valleys to Margam and also as a diversionary route for the SWML, with a reversal at Tondu. The signal box was closed in October 1983. (Michael Hale/GW Trust)

Cwmffos level crossing (now Trainman Operated) ½ mile before Cefn Junction is seen here with 60040 on 24 August 2014. (S. Warr)

junction from 2m 31ch to Cefn Jct. SB (opened in 1898) at 2m 47ch and on to 2m 51ch along the line to Pyle. The Port Talbot branch was doubled from the junction for 15 chains and for a further 15ch in 1930.

Approaching the new junction from Tondu, a new SB was opened at Ffoes Bank in 1898, 22ch east of Cefn Jct. box and was closed in 1930, when the loop approaching the junction was shortened by 5ch. The colliery, which had a connection into the PTR line, was closed in about 1918.

The line between Cefn Jct. and Port Talbot (into the Steel Company of Wales) became known as the Ogmore Vale Extension (OVE) line. In September 1965, the junction was singled, the loops on both lines being removed. In August 1966, the junction was moved east by a chain. In November 1973, the Cefn Jct. to Porthcawl section was taken out of use and the loop on the Port Talbot line, which was now the through line, reinstated. This situation lasted until 7 October 1983 when Cefn Junction box was closed and the loop on the OVE removed. The section then became single line throughout which still pertains. Cefn Junction SB has been the subject of a local community project (Y Cefn Gwyrdd) and has been preserved in situ.

Waterhall Sidings SB on 16 April 1960. The Signal Box, though on the PTR, is of GW origin and 1909 vintage. It was named Waterhall Sidings to avoid confusion with Waterhall Junction in the Cardiff area. (Michael Hale/GW Trust)

Waterhall Sidings on 16 April 1960. Here the curve from Pyle joined the single track OVE which had a group of sidings here that served local collieries. The Northern part of the curve was lifted in 1958 and its course later obliterated by new housing. (Michael Hale/GW Trust)

Newlands SB on 16 April 1960. The OVE became double track at Newlands and passed over the South Wales Main Line to enter the Margam complex. On the right here, a connection comes in from the East side of the Main Line. The Box closed from 12 April 1973 when the line was singled, the line remaining in use today as necessary. (Michael Hale/GW Trust)

Now to 1983 and a Sunday main line diversion due to work on an embankment between Port Talbot and Bridgend involving diversion via Tondu. At the end of the tokenless block section from Margam Moors to Cefn Jct, here the 9.30am Swansea to Paddington takes the token from the Cefn Jct. signalman for the section from there to Tondu Middle. Such diversions have now been changed to replacement bus services. (Stephen Miles)

Between Cefn Junction and Pyle existed Bedford Road (Brickworks) Level Crossing which is seen here in the distance together with the resident Keeper's House on 19 October 1968.

An original Llynvi & Ogmore Railway quarter milepost located outside Cefn Junction Signal Box September 1998. After closure, the Box was taken over by a local amenity group called Y Cefn Gwrydd. The building was restored so that it could be used as a meeting place and display centre.
(Stuart Davies)

Cefn Junction on 18 June 1962. 6431 working the 7.25pm Auto from Porthcawl crosses 4251 on 8T80 7.10pm Tondu to Margam New Yard. This 'Jumbo' service had been introduced in February with the opening of the New Yard at Margam. Routed by Kenfig Hill and Pyle in preference to the PTR Route avoided a reversal. (Garth Tilt)

4251 in the previous photo continues on its way leaving the banker at Cefn Junction. Before it can return home 7732 will have to wait until the 7.25pm Porthcawl Auto with 6419 in charge, clears section at Velin Vach. (Garth Tilt)

KENFIG HILL

Kenfig Hill station was located between Cefn Jct. and Pyle at 3m 64ch from Tondu. The station was called Cefn until 1 August 1885. There was a LC at the east end of the single platform with the SB located towards the west end of the platform. The SB was closed in 1929 when the connections into a siding at the west end of the station were controlled by the East and West Ground Frames. The siding and GFs were taken out of use in March 1950. The station and goods facility were closed on 5th May 1958. Located between Tondu and Pyle, Kenfig Hill only had a sparse passenger service when stock was being moved between Tondu and Pyle and back, the main service being concentrated between Pyle and Porthcawl. The lack of patronage on the unattractive service led to its closure in 1958. There were various other industrial concerns at Kenfig Hill but these were accessed off the Ogmore Vale Extension of the Port Talbot Railway between Cefn Jct. and Margam.

Kenfig Hill was located between Cefn Jct. and Pyle on the L&O line, 3¾ miles from Tondu. This view of the single platform and staff, looking west towards Pyle, dates from the early years of the century. There was a LC just east of the station with the signal box on the west end of the platform. (Lens of Sutton)

Kenfig Hill looking towards Tondu on 14 March 1965. (Garth Tilt)

Bryndu Crossing between Kenfig Hill and Pyle viewed looking towards Tondu on 18 June 1965. The Crossing Keeper's dwelling to the right. (Garth Tilt)

At ¾ miles on the approach to Pyle, trains from/to Tondu passed under the South Wales Main Line as seen here with 6431 on the 7.25pm Porthcawl to Tondu Auto on 18 June 1962. This part of the Porthcawl line closed on 18 November 1973 and Down Mineral trains to Margam had no option but to traverse the PTR line from Cefn Junction. (Garth Tilt)

Ton Phillip at Kenfig Hill was accessed off the Ogmore Vale Extension line from Cefn Jct. to Margam. This view (c1910) show staff from the colliery at a pre-arranged session as one man has brought his dog and others probably their children. The wagon promotes the colliery as producing gas and house coal.

PYLE

A plan for 1876 shows a single line running from Cefn into Pyle which previously crossed the South Wales Main Line (SWML) as a flat crossing. Then, in November 1876, the alignment of this line was considerably changed to provide an underbridge crossing of the main line further east. A new SB, Pyle No. 1, opened in November 1876 linking the Llynfi & Ogmore line with the SWML. This long link line was much shortened in March 1882 to deviate closer to the L&O station, with the ground thrown up used to house two loop sidings, with a facing connection from the down SWML into them and to double the L&O line approaching the doubled junction, becoming single again to access the L&O platform.

By 1900, the two loop sidings had disappeared and been replaced by a double line connection from the SWML into the L&O to provide for through running from the main line to Porthcawl. In 1912 the junction between the main and branch lines was again altered this time to provide a diamond junction. A second platform was added on the branch and the line doubled to just beyond the Porthcawl end. With the doubling of the branch, the alignment of the original single line was moved south immediately beyond the branch platforms. A siding, stop-blocked at the east end, was also provided on the branch east of the crossover.

A view from the platform footbridge at Pyle looking east on Friday 21 September 1962. The South Wales Main Line passes to the left and is part of Stormy Bank, a three-mile eastbound gradient of 1 in 93 which presented a challenge to the progress of heavy freight trains which often required banking. Straight ahead is the L&O Line to Tondu which soon becomes single track. A double scissors junction affords connections to and from both routes. Note the demounted veteran passenger coaches at the end of the up main line platform. (Bluebell Archive)

This view taken on 1 August 1958 of the Loading Dock and Cattle Pens at Pyle shows the curve leading to the PTR at Waterhall Junction, where it joined the Margam Moors to Cefn Jct. line. The chord line which had a running loop and two sidings at the Pyle end closed in 1948 and was then used for wagon storage. In this picture the only wagons there were engineer's wagons of ballast. (Michael Hale/GW Trust)

10 September 1951
at the bottom of Stormy Bank, a view from the Down Main platform at Pyle looking East towards Cardiff. (Kidderminster Railway Museum)

Pyle East Signalbox
which controlled a double scissors layout enabling access to/from the Porthcawl branch in the Cardiff direction and to/from Tondu in the Swansea direction, as seen on 28 July 1963. With running lines both sides of the box two nameplates would be fitted one either side (not unique but uncommon).
(Kidderminster Railway Museum)

4135 in GW livery at Pyle with a through working to Porthcawl off the mainline on 26 August 1940. (R.C. Riley collection/Kidderminster Railway Museum)

A view dating from 10 September 1951 of the Pyle-Porthcawl service when worked by the small prairie 4400 Class, due to the severe curves on the line between Tondu and Porthcawl. The view shows 4404 standing under the footbridge. There were only eleven of this class of small Prairies and they had a long association with Tondu and the Porthcawl branch in particular. 4404 was the longest serving and at least one was based at Tondu almost continuously between 1919 and 1952 until the advent of their larger auto-fitted sisters of the 4575 sub-class. (H.C. Casserley)

Dating from 10 September 1951 when the Pyle-Porthcawl services were worked by the small prairie 4400 Class, due to the severe curves on the line between Tondu and Porthcawl. The view shows 4404 standing at the up platform, having run around its arriving train and will either start its next service to Porthcawl from this platform. (H.C. Casserley)

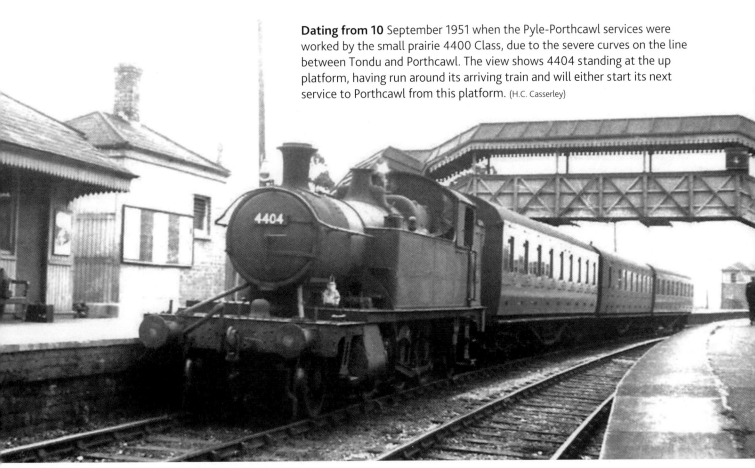

4406 arrives at the up platform with the three coach 12.40pm Porthcawl to Tondu on 13 September 1952. This was the last of the morning turns and it is probable that the afternoon turn would be worked by 4408 which was also based at Tondu for the Porthcawl workings at this time. (R.J. Buckley/Initial Photographics)

The Porthcawl Branch seen from the road overbridge at the west end of Pyle station. 5555 propels an Auto Train consisting of former Taff Vale trailers W6422 (TV No. 79) and W2506 (TV No. 353) heading for the seaside on Monday 4 July 1955. There were three pairs of these trailers which unusually had a corridor connection between the two vehicles and all three were to be found at Tondu at this late stage in their careers. This pair ended on Saturday 10 September 1955 at the end of the Summer Timetable. The Porthcawl branch was doubled in 1924 as far as Cornelly, largely due to the amount of summer weekend traffic. (D.K. Jones Collection)

Tondu's 5555 on 9 August 1958 in a typical 'fore and aft' four coach auto train. Two four coach auto trains worked on the Porthcawl branch on Summer Saturdays at this time. With the closure of Abergwynfi in 1960, these engines were replaced by the less powerful 6400 Class. (A.E. Bennett)

Saturday 16 April
1960 and 3668 with
a three-coach train of
conventional stock,
enters Pyle at 10.12am
with a service
from Porthcawl.
(Porthcawl Museum)

Pyle with 6419 and
Auto for Porthcawl
sometime in 1963.
(Garth Tilt)

Two views of former Abercynon engine, 6435 with the 9.40am to Porthcawl, starting from the up platform on 1 September 1962. The pictures show both the platforms on the Porthcawl branch in some detail. During the Summer holidays some privileged schoolboys used the water tank as a private swimming pool until a blockage occurred, the cause of which was found to be a Conger Eel. (W.G. Sumner)

Looking towards Stormy Down on what was clearly a stormy day on 18 June 1962 seen from the 7.25pm Auto from Porthcawl to Tondu with 6431 in charge at the rear. (Garth Tilt)

Though it is July, two coaches now suffice on this auto formation as 6419 stands at the up platform in charge of the 7.15pm from Porthcawl on 9 July 1963. Two more trips and then the 9.15pm from Porthcawl ran Main Line to Bridgend and worked a service to Cymmer. (W.G. Sumner)

Saturday 18 June 1962 and 6431 with the 7.25pm Auto from Porthcawl approaches Pyle where 4121 waits with the 7.35 Pyle to Porthcawl. The latter faces two round trips to Porthcawl before leaving at 9.15 with a service to Bridgend. It will then form the 11.10pm to Cymmer returning to Tondu by midnight. (Garth Tilt)

HEOL Y SHEET

Heol y Sheet SB and LC at 6m.55ch. from Tondu was the junction at which the trailing Pyle West Loop, the direct route from Neath and Swansea, joined the line from Tondu. It was opened in March 1947 and closed on 1st February 1965. The box existed before the building of the Loop but only to operate the LC and received a new frame in 1938.

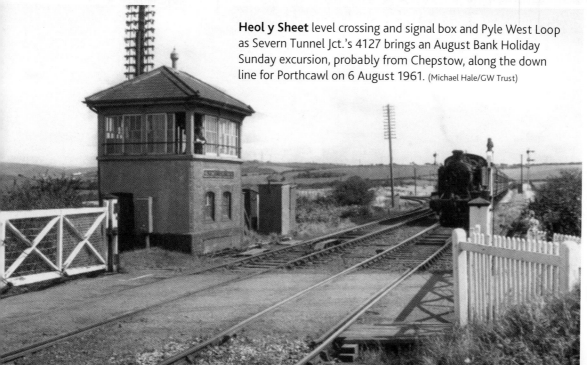

Heol y Sheet level crossing and signal box and Pyle West Loop as Severn Tunnel Jct.'s 4127 brings an August Bank Holiday Sunday excursion, probably from Chepstow, along the down line for Porthcawl on 6 August 1961. (Michael Hale/GW Trust)

Pyle West Junction as seen on 14 March 1965. The link to Heol y Sheet was commissioned in 1947 and allowed Swansea services direct access to the Porthcawl branch. (Garth Tilt)

The Standard 4MTs were handsome locomotives and very popular even with Crews reared on pure Great Western steeds. So no apologies for another shot of 80133 as she approaches Heol y Sheet on 3 June 1963 with the 5.30 from Neath to Porthcawl. (Garth Tilt)

The 7.25pm Porthcawl to Tondu with 6431 at Heol y Sheet literally heads straight for home on 18 June 1962. (Garth Tilt)

CORNELLY

A plan for 1898 shows a single line running past the limestone quarry siding which consisted of a 16ch. loop alongside the running line. South of this were a variety of sidings being converted from tramways and tramways themselves to Pantmawr and Cornelly Quarries, the Pantmawr line being converted in 1904. Originally, the sidings were owned by North's Navigation but from 1904, the lines were classed as being linked to the railway and a PSA was granted to E.R. Thomas and to L. Railton in 1910, passing to Cornelly Quarry Co. Ltd. in June 1917.

In May 1924, the single line was realigned and doubled from Cornelly SB at 7¼ mp back to Pyle. In April 1927, Grove Quarry was added to the complex with their own PSA with a new loading dock and tramway in 1929, further extended in 1930. In August 1930, the Cornelly Quarry PSA passed to Guest Keen & Baldwin Iron & Steel Co. Ltd.

New nests of sidings and a loading ramp were added at the west end of the complex, in place of the Grove sidings, these being in the name of SCOW who had a PSA from February 1946. Cornelly SB was rebuilt following a fire in 1958 and closed on 1 February 1965, when the freight service to Porthcawl ceased, the limestone from Cornelly then passing by road. The Pyle to Porthcawl branch was then completely closed, the passenger service having been removed at the end of the summer season on 9 September 1963.

A view of the signal box (renewed in 1958) and level crossing at Cornelly on 6 August 1961 showing the end of the double line section and part of the complex of sidings owned by SCOW for the loading of their limestone traffic. A derailment at Pyle on 6 April 1964 led to the diversion of a number of Passenger trains onto the Porthcawl branch. Trains reversed at Cornelly and were re-engined to continue their journey, most worked by Western Type 4s. (Michael Hale/GW Trust)

The idyllic setting of Cornelly level crossing and signal box seen from the roadway on 28 July 1963. The three arms of the bracket signal permit entry (from right to left) to the single running line, the siding alongside the running line and the SCOW sidings. (P.J. Garland/Roger Carpenter)

Cornelly looking towards Pyle on 14 March 1965. The Porthcawl Branch had been doubled from here to Pyle in 1924. (Garth Tilt)

Pantmawr Limestone Quarry at Cornelly looking towards Porthcawl. This was the major source of originating goods traffic on the branch, the Limestone being used at Port Talbot Steelworks. (Garth Tilt)

Cornelly's impressive Three Doll Bracket Signal controls access onto the single-track branch (right) from here to Porthcawl. The parallel track alongside is a siding. 14 March 1965. (Garth Tilt)

NOTTAGE

Nottage Halt was located at 8m 46ch from Tondu on the single line between Cornelly and Porthcawl. It was opened for public use on 14 July 1924, having previously been the unadvertised Porthcawl Golfers' Platform. Ten chains west of the station was a 62 yard long tunnel, added to by spark troughs. A clause written into the Llynvi Valley Railway (LVR) Act of 1852 prevented any device other than animal power from passing through the lands of the Rt. Hon. Charlotte Guest and Rev. Henry Knight. Nottage Tunnel was constructed in order to prevent damage to their property arising from smoke and sparks. Until 1861, steam locomotives went only as far as Pyle. The 62 yard tunnel was cut through solid rock and at each end, steel sheets were erected for additional deflection.

Nottage Halt had only a limited service to/from Pyle whereby trains called on request and was not served by Swansea trains. In the Down direction, alighting passengers were to notify the guard at Pyle; passengers wishing to join Up trains gave a handsignal to the driver as the train approached.

Nottage Halt looking North towards Pyle on 28 July 1963. The halt was on the single line that started west of Cornelly and trains called on request. It was opened in July 1924 and was previously the unadvertised Porthcawl Golfers' Platform.
(P.J. Garland/R.S. Carpenter)

Ten chains west of Nottage Halt was the 62 yard long Tunnel and Spark deflector plates, with two views on 28 July 1963.
(Both P.J. Garland/ R.S. Carpenter)

Nottage Halt looking towards Porthcawl on 1st September 1962. (W.G. Sumner)

A stopping service from Swansea to Porthcawl passes through Nottage Halt behind Landore's 5631 on 16 April 1960. (Michael Hale/GW Trust)

PORTHCAWL

A plan for 1875 shows a single line running into Porthcawl from Pyle with a loop on the south side. Off the loop was a PSA into a quarry owned by the Cardiff Silica Firebrick Co., with a PSA dated the last day of 1875. In April 1877, this passed to Messrs. Howell & Rees and in June 1900 to P.L. Noel, before passing to J.C. Coath (trading as Howell & Rees) from July 1913, becoming known as Coath's Quarry on a plan for 1916, remaining as such until closure January 1928.

Eight chains west was the single Porthcawl passenger platform and station, with a loop running alongside the running line, a LC and SB at the west end. West of the station were five long sidings stop-blocked at the west end, two of which continued into the Dock area, with other sidings leading into the western end of the Dock. The Dock was divided into the North and West Quays along the top side of the dock and the East Quay which ran along the whole of the bottom side. The main dock ran west into a Basin which led to the open sea. Two main discharge points for coal traffic (tips) were located along the North Quay but sidings ran alongside each Quay as well as curving east.

A plan for 1898 shows that the station's passenger platform had been doubled, the original platform also having been extended. The SB was shown on the north side of the LC and had been replaced in 1895 and 1897. A Goods Yard and Shed were located west of the LC at the north end of the sidings. In 1895, a third tip and access road were built on the North Quay together with four additional storage sidings for shipment coal wagons.

With the opening of more modern docks at Barry and Port Talbot, Porthcawl Docks became surplus to requirements and the GWR closed them in 1898. A process of

A 56XX heads past Nottage Halt with a service from Swansea in this undated view

recovery of the surrounding sidings, draining and filling in the Dock began which would last for many years.

An excursion platform was built west of the station, alongside the northernmost siding in 1909/10. A variety of private sidings existed on the docks, including a Gas Works, Sand & Gravel company and R.S. Hayes Wagon Repairs, the last more appropriate in coal shipment days. All these were removed during the 1920s and 30s.

In 1916, a new station was built at Porthcawl some 20 chains west of the old station on land reclaimed from the previous dock sidings and tip roads. The three new platforms were joined at the west end and enclosed two stop-blocked tracks with a third serving the south face. Thus, the north platform was single, but the south was an island. The previous holding sidings for wagons of shipment

traffic were re-planned and slewed to become holding sidings for excursion trains of which up to a dozen could be accommodated together with a triangle leading off the outer face of the island platform to enable engines to be turned.

Like Barry Island, Porthcawl became a day-tripper resort with day excursions from the Valleys and also main line origins. It was common for up to about 10 excursions to run on weekends and bank holidays, though 4-6-0 engines on main line excursions had to change engines at Cardiff to a 2-6-0 because of branch restrictions west of Pyle.

Porthcawl became a casualty of the Beeching Plan and the passenger service was withdrawn at the end of the summer season on 9 September 1963. Freight services were removed on 1 February 1965 when the whole branch from Pyle to Porthcawl was closed and recovered.

Taken in 1913, this view shows the layout at Porthcawl beyond the level crossing prior to the station's reconstruction and relocation in 1916.

This 1915 view shows work being carried out to fill in the Inner Harbour in preparation for the redevelopment of the passenger facilities at Porthcawl. An open cab pannier tank is in charge of hopper wagons full of the filling material being used. Six of the previous holding sidings for wagons of shipment traffic were retained to become holding sidings for excursion trains. Class 4200 locomotives hauled trains of waste slag from Ebbw Vale to fill the inner dock. (Porthcawl Museum)

Porthcawl Harbour and breakwater.

The first station at Porthcawl dating from 1875, located further north than the final station, opened in 1916. (Lens of Sutton)

A group of passengers stand on the down platform as a 1076 Class Buffalo 0-6-0ST waits to cross the level crossing at the north end of the platform. (Lens of Sutton/Porthcawl Museum)

These two views taken on 14 March 1965 show the section of line between the old station and the new. By now, the line to Porthcawl had closed, but this gives a clear indication of the extent of the layout provided. The centre lines are the main lines in and out of the station, those on the left and right being for storage of empty stock and remade from previous dock lines, also provided for beyond the level crossing where the previous dock lines were converted into the main area for holding empty stock off excursions. (Garth Tilt)

Paddle Steamer
Bristol Queen was in the P&A Campbell (Red Funnel) Fleet that operated regular sailings in the Bristol Channel during summer months and is seen here on the approach to Porthcawl on 13 June 1967.
(Porthcawl Museum)

An aerial view of Porthcawl showing the proximity of the railway to the coast and that of the town to the railway.

The interior of the booking hall as at opening of the new station in 1916.
(Porthcawl Museum)

A view of the new station building frontage at Porthcawl in 1916.
(Porthcawl Museum)

The layout of the platforms at the new station in 1916. (Porthcawl Museum)

A 1950s view towards Pyle with excursion stock stabled in the carriage (previously coal hoist) sidings. (D.K. Jones collection)

Another view of the original station at Porthcawl c1916 just before the new station opened south of this view with a level crossing in between. (Porthcawl Museum)

The 45XXs began working to Porthcawl early and here Tondu based 4539 is seen alongside the Signal Box in 1916. (LGRP)

The line continued beyond the end of platform 3 to provide the facility for incoming engines to access the connection to run round via a triangle which brought them back to the north end of the station. Porthcawl No. 2 ground frame (right of centre) controlled the access to the triangle. №1 ground frame operated the crossover between platforms 1 and 2. (P.J. Garland/R.S. Carpenter)

Porthcawl was vested with a triangle for turning locomotives. Porthcawl No. 2 Ground Frame operation gave access to its divergence from the outer platform (No. 3). The other corner had a headshunt long enough to accommodate a 63XX but operated by handpoint. Fortunately, this unimposing facility has been captured here on 14 March 1965. (Garth Tilt)

Porthcawl No. 2 Ground Frame controlling access to the triangle for turning engines with the stop block denoting the end of the line.
(P.J. Garland/R.S. Carpenter)

A view of the station from the water tower on 9 June 1960.
(P.J. Garland/R.S. Carpenter)

PORTHCAWL 1960

Line Closed 1.2.1965

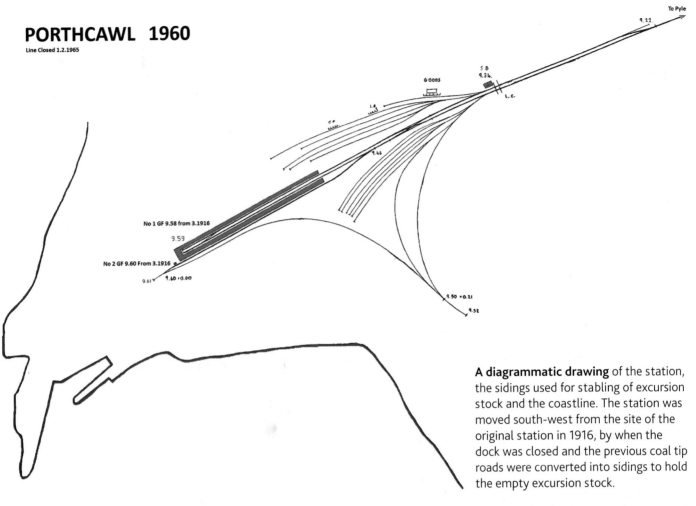

A **diagrammatic drawing** of the station, the sidings used for stabling of excursion stock and the coastline. The station was moved south-west from the site of the original station in 1916, by when the dock was closed and the previous coal tip roads were converted into sidings to hold the empty excursion stock.

A **view of** the platforms from the stop blocks on 28 July 1963. (P.J. Garland/R.S. Carpenter)

A view looking south-west towards the station from the site of the original station where the controlling signal box and level crossing were located. The loop line left of centre brought engines back out onto the main line after turning. Other sidings in this area were used for stabling of empty stock. (P.J. Garland/R.S. Carpenter)

Porthcawl Signal Box with a glimpse of the modest Goods Shed on the left as on 28 July 1963. (P.J. Garland/R.S. Carpenter)

Canton's 3394
Australia with an excursion at Porthcawl in the summer of 1923.

Whit Sunday (9 June 1957) and the usual bank holiday excursions had worked to Porthcawl. Here, 6362 draws its stock forward before backing into the station ready for the return home. Each movement to/from the station and to/from the sidings involved closure to road traffic of the Level Crossing seen in the bottom of the picture. This scene is typical of Porthcawl's railway in the summer season with the sidings capable of holding up to eleven trains and oh! It's raining! Foreign crews were relieved on arrival by Tondu men based there for the day to keep the locos in steam until the return journeys, the foreign crews no doubt sampling the delights of Fulgoni's Ice Cream (a Welsh speciality) or a liquid alternative in the Knight's Arms just around the corner from the station. 6677, 5676, 4107, 3680 and 8104 worked in on excursions that day and stand at the head of their trains in the sidings. (Michael Hale/GW Trust)

Porthcawl Glory Days. Saturday 5th June 1960 with seven excursion trains. 6366 of Swindon Shed and not fitted with outside steam pipes, draws forward out of the sidings with the coaches of return excursion X54. 6634+6675 are backing X52 for Pontypool Road via the Vale of Neath into Platform 3. Other excursions are also visible including, 4134 with X37, 5169 and 5643. 5643 and 6634 both passed into preservation. Imagine the effect with each movement between yard and station having to pass over the level crossing twice. Porthcawl Signalmen must have developed very muscular arms. (S. Rickard/J&J Colln)

6410 arriving at Porthcawl in the afternoon of 30 June 1962 with a three coach auto from Pyle as the signalman takes the token for the single line section from Cornelly. (F.K. Davies)

Having worked in on the lunchtime train from Cardiff, 3100 at Porthcawl on 29 July 1955 with Coney Beach in the background. The morning business train through to Cardiff at 7.50am ex-Porthcawl arrived at 8.40am and was the reason for 3100's allocation to Tondu, thereafter working other services between Cardiff and Porthcawl. She replaced a long line of individual 'Bulldogs' for the same purpose which arguably worked an early example of a commuter service. (Ian L. Wright)

4177 and excursion train from the Cardiff Valleys, berthed in the Carriage Sidings awaiting their return journey 9 August 1958. (A.E. Bennett)

6435 with Auto-coaches W241 W242 forming the West Glamorgan/ Monmouthshire Railway Societies' charter 8 June 1963.

On a bright Summer's day 4166 and 6361 stand with their empty stock from the Cardiff Valleys and Vale of Neath line in the Carriage Sidings and Goods Yard respectively on 30 June 1962. (F.K. Davies)

A close up view of former TVR Auto set W6422W & W2506W at the end of their last Summer Season working services between Pyle and Porthcawl, standing condemned at Porthcawl on 29 July 1955. (Ian L. Wright)

In the days of the 4400 Class operation of the working to Porthcawl, 4404 runs into No. 1 platform with a three-coach service from Pyle on 10 September 1951. (H.C. Casserley)

Tondu's 8446 stands at Platform 1 at the head of a return service on 29 July 1955. (Ian L. Wright)

One of the engines allocated to Tondu for auto working replacing the 4575s was 6431 seen here running into Platform 1 at Porthcawl with the 10.50am service from Pyle on 21 August 1962. (S. Rickard/J&J Collection)

A view of the north end of the platforms each with a bracket signal controlling exit. The water tower is shown to good advantage with an excursion train in the siding behind.

Just to prove the Big Boys sometimes came to the seaside; 4287 (probably covering for a failure or shortage) waits to return with an excursion on 15 September 1946. 4286 had worked similarly on 5 September 1962. Fortunately at that time of year, no steam heating would have been required!

6435 and 6361 framed by three Double Bracket Signals at Porthcawl on 8 June 1963. 6435 with Auto-coaches W241 W242 was in charge of the Mid Glamorgan Railtour run on behalf of West Glamorgan/Monmouthshire Railway Societies. (F.K. Davies)

4107 (allocated to Landore 1.57 to 6.60) has turned after arrival at 1.17 with the 12.15 from Swansea and waits to return at 1.35. An Auto service arrived at 12.55 returning to Tondu at 1.10 and the 12.20 from Cardiff arriving at 1.26 explains the Swansea's accommodation in Platform 3.

The largest main line engine allowed on the Porthcawl branch was the 2-6-0 4300 Class and excursions often had to change engines at Cardiff to this type of engine. Summer Saturdays saw a through train from the Bristol Division timetabled to work through to Porthcawl and it was normal for a 43XX engine to work through on this. Here 6364 of St. Philip's Marsh, Bristol shed arrives at Porthcawl on 14 July 1962, with 1T24, the 9.55am Weston-super-Mare to Porthcawl stopping service: The return working was the 2.10pm Porthcawl - Cardiff. (Porthcawl Museum)

6361 of Aberdare waits for departure with a return excursion over the Vale of Neath to Pontypool Road, 8 June 1963. (F.K. Davies)

8 June 1963 and 80133 with the 5.05pm from Swansea waits to return there from Porthcawl at 6.40pm. The locomotive has been turned by means of the triangle that led from the outer platform and bordered the carriage sidings. (F.K. Davies)

9 August 1958 and on arrival at Porthcawl, the driver walks with a sense of purpose from his cab at one end of the train to that at the front casting a careful eye over his charge (5555) in doing so. (A.E. Bennett)

Porthcawl September 1962; a DMU forms the 6.55pm to Newport but the 6.32pm to Swansea has a more exotic charge in the form of a Fowler 2-6-4T 42388. The former LNWR Shed at Swansea Paxton Street had closed in August 1959 and some of its locomotive stud transferred to Swansea East Dock. From 12 June 1961, Swansea Landore was closed to steam, its remaining charges and associated services transferred to Neath (Court Sart) and Llanelli. Some contrivance by the respective shed foremen at East Dock and Neath must have occurred to give rise to this exclusive event. (F.K. Davies)

The paintwork of Auto-trailer W241 says it all. This is Saturday 9 September 1963, the last day of passenger services at Porthcawl. 6434 leading Auto-trailers W246 and W241 shown here, had the dubious honour of working the last Tondu afternoon turn on the branch. The last trains however, were at 7.45pm to Cardiff and 8.10pm to Swansea. Remaining until November 1962, Auto-trailers W241, W245, W246 and W256 were the last of their kind at Tondu but only W241 was to the classic design, the others being conversions from non-corridor brakes.

Staff at the original station at the turn of the century. (Porthcawl Museum)

Porthcawl Station staff 1916. The stationmaster sits centre no doubt proud of his new station. (Porthcawl Museum)

**Porthcawl staff
in** the 1930s.
(Porthcawl Museum)

**Porthcawl station
staff** in 1961.
(Porthcawl Museum)

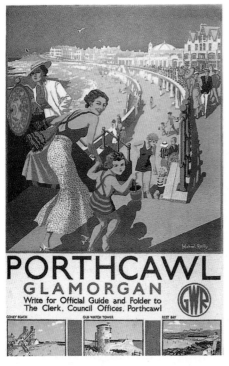

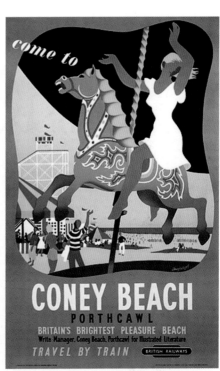

Posters promoting the various delights of Porthcawl produced by the GW and BR(W) Publicity Departments throughout the years.

CHAPTER 4

GILFACH GOCH BRANCH

BLACKMILL

Also covered in Chapter 1 Ogmore Branch

Not far beyond the viaduct carrying the Cardiff & Ogmore Rly., an 1875 drawing shows a siding going off north at Dimbath but never developed. Whether this was intended to be a shorter route to Gilfach Goch seems possible. By 1893, the area had been developed into a loop siding with another siding going off along the line of the original while another stop block siding ran parallel with the loop. A PSA dated December 1893 in favour of Leyshon & Lilwall, replacing an earlier PSA, seems to have covered provision of a tramway rather than a siding but by the end of 1895, it had all been closed and soon recovered.

A few chains further east, on both sides of the line, were connections into and out of the Glynogwr Colliery, also known as Tynygraig or Cwmogwr. Opened by the Llantwit Coal Co., a drawing for 1874 shows a connection on the north side of the running line, leading to sidings which were to be extended under a PSA dated November 1876 granted to Henry Kirkhouse who was to re-open the colliery, but all had been removed by 1881.

A drawing for 1913 shows a tramway on the other side of the line where, in March 1913, a PSA was granted to the Glenavon Garw Collieries Ltd, to which a shoot was added in July 1914 in the name of J. Bryant, passing to John Beamand in February 1916. A plan for 1917 shows the tramway had crossed an overbridge to the north side of the line in the name of Beamand from June 1916. From January 1917, the tramway was in the name of the Tynygraig Colliery Co. Ltd., and from May 1930 was owned by the Cwmogwr Colliery Co. Ltd. In June 1935, the colliery went into receivership and the siding agreement was terminated in December 1935, when the undertaking was wound up.

Approaching Hendreforgan, there was a colliery called Caradog Vale on the south side of the line, accessed by two long sidings. A PSA was granted in February 1877 to Jones Bros. This passed through a J. Humby and H.R. Scott before being taken over by the Caradog Vale Colliery Co. in June 1900, the Groeswen & Caradog Collieries Ltd. in July 1902 and the South Wales United Collieries in December 1903 before returning to H.R. Scott in June 1912 and being terminated in December 1928. Before this, the colliery had been re-opened as Graig Las Colliery in mid-1928 and the company of that name ran it until closure in April 1934.

HENDREFORGAN

The line from Blackmill through Hendreforgan ran on east to Gellyrhaidd Jct. where it met the Ely Valley Line from Llantrisant and Coedely north to Tonyrefail and Penygraig. The Gilfach Goch line was a continuation of the line from Llantrisant and connected with the line from Blackmill at Gilfach Jct., involving a reversal at Hendreforgan for trains between Bridgend and Gilfach Goch.

A plan for 1875, the year of opening of the passenger station, shows a single line platform between the single lines from Blackmill and that from Gilfach Jct. to Gilfach Goch, which ran parallel from the west and the line on to Gellyrhaidd Jct. to the east. R.A. Cooke states in his layout for Hendreforgan that much remains unknown or unconfirmed about the branches (and thereby the sidings) in this area.

Gilfach Jct. lay at 6m 11ch from Blackmill, 1m 58ch from Gellyrhaidd Jct. and was a starting mileage (0.00) on to Gilfach Goch. The SB originally stood on the north side of the line at the east end of the single platform but in later years was moved to the south side of the line at the west end of the platform. It closed in June 1957 with the closure of the line to Blackmill.

On the line from Hendreforgan to Gilfach Goch, a plan for 1875 shows a long loop running west from Gilfach Jct. for holding trains off the branch, while on the Gellyrhaidd Jct. side of the station were two long sidings on the north side of the line. As the line swung north towards Gilfach Goch, a trailing siding, probably connected to a colliery, was in existence until 1881 but nothing is known as to ownership.

Trains from Bridgend and Tondu to Gilfach Goch reversed at Hendreforgan to proceed via Gilfach Junction up the branch to Gilfach Goch. In this west-facing view at Hendreforgan (looking to Blackmill) on 5 April 1958, it can be seen that a siding had been created on the former Blackmill alignment accessed by a Ground Frame which had replaced the Signal Box in June 1957. Track-lifting of the Blackmill Branch and all the other sidings at Hendreforgan took place in August 1957. The Gilfach to Gellyrhaidd Branch closed in March 1962. (Michael Hale/GW Trust)

Hendreforgan looking towards Blackmill. The Gilfach line branches off to the right of the three Doll Bracket in the distance; the line to Blackmill diverges to its left at the end of the platform. The route to Blackmill was closed in September 1930 so the date of this photograph is before then. (Graham Croad)

Gellyrhaidd Jcn looking north on 20 September 1962. Alongside the signal box 9778 stands on the remnant of the Blackmill line awaiting its next banking duty to Clydach. A short stretch of the Blackmill line was left in place after track-lifting in 1957 to enable locomotives to reach the water column. (C.H.A. Townley)

GILFACH GOCH

A plan of the south Gilfach area for 1876 shows Gilfach Colliery on the north side of the line, owned by the Glamorgan Coal Co. In a plan for 1880, the colliery is shown as the Lower Gilfach Colliery with sidings extending back to where the passenger station would be built to open in 1881 at 1m.12ch. from Gilfach Jct. (Hendreforgan), with a through line to the Gilfach Goch collieries, north of the station. There was a stop-blocked bay line on the south side with a run-round loop south of that.

A plan for 1915 shows a new goods loop and sidings south of the station with a Goods Yard and Shed with two collieries now shown directly north of the station. The first of these was Etna Colliery, originally known as Dylas Isha Colliery and opened in 1901 to access the Rhondda No. 2 seam. By 1910, it was owned by the Etna Colliery Co., a PSA was granted in July 1915 to W. Perch & Co. Ltd., passing to the Blaenclydach Colliery Co. by 1918, when still known as Dylas Isha and to Etna Colliery Co. Ltd in January 1921, finally to the Glenavon Garw Collieries Ltd. in May 1923 before terminating with the closure of the colliery in April 1929. 300 men were employed at the pit and Etna.

On the south side of the line in the same area was the Glenogwr (or Gibbs) Colliery, opened in 1909 by Robert Gibb, the PSA passing to the Glynogwr Collieries Ltd. in August 1910 and to Glenavon Garw Collieries in April 1911. The colliery produced manufacturing and house coal from the Nos 2 and 3 Rhondda seams, finally closing in 1949, the manpower transferred to Tymawr colliery north of Pontypridd to open up a new seam. The colliery was divided into north and south on the 1915 plan.

In 1934, the Glenavon Garw Collieries Ltd. controlled six collieries employing over 3,300 miners, producing 850,000 tons of coal annually and became a subsidiary of the Ocean Coal Co.

The station was originally named Gilfach and became Gilfach Goch on 30 June 1928 but did not last long. It was closed when the passenger service on the branch from Blackmill was terminated on 22 September 1930. North of the station on the north side was a one-track goods shed and a yard siding with a loop north of the running line. This survived until 5 June 1961 which would have meant that a general freight service survived on the branch until then, albeit served from Llantrisant.

At the end of the branch at 2m 8ch from Gilfach Jct. (at Hendreforgan) a plan for 1875 shows Gilfach Goch Upper and Lower Collieries on the north side of the running line with coke ovens and sidings also on the south side with tramways extending north beyond the end of the running line. The colliery was opened by the Glamorgan Coal Co. during the mid-1870s and was also known as the Glamorgan Colliery. The Upper Colliery was towards the end of the branch with the Lower some 500 yards to the south. Both pits produced mining clay and house coal and consisted of a shaft and drifts. Lower Gilfach Colliery closed in the 1890s whilst the Upper Colliery carried on producing with about 175 miners in 1918 but was shown only as a pumping station in 1920.

On the south side of the line, almost at the end of the branch was Dinas Main Colliery with tramway-fed coke ovens further south. This was the first pit in Gilfach Goch, sunk in 1868 by Evan Evans who acquired the mineral rights of a considerable area of land in the area in the early 1860s.

A short distance south was the Britannic Trane Pit, sunk by the Dinas Main Coal Co. in 1887, with their first PSA dated September 1896. It was known as the Dinas Steam pit. The Dinas Main Coal Co. sank two deep shafts between 1894-6 to the steam coal levels, known as Dinas New Pits and these became known as the Britannic Merthyr Colliery. The Merthyr element was probably because a large number of the miners had come to the area from Merthyr when the pits were being opened by Evan Evans and they lived in an area known as Evanstown. There were almost 700 men employed at the Britannic Steam Coal pit and Dinas Main House Coal pit.

By 1900, plans of the area show a Gilfach Goch Colliery Platform for miners' use at about 1m 70ch but this was not shown on the 1920 or subsequent plans. The Dinas Main House Coal Pit was closed in 1907 after a fatal explosion but Dinas Main Level was immediately opened to continue to work the house coal seams.

By 1904, the Britannic was owned by the Britannic Merthyr Colliery Co. Ltd., and in 1908 employed over 700 men. The Company was formed by David Alfred Thomas who later became the first Viscount Rhondda. The Britannic (Dinas Trane) Steam Pit was deepened in 1911-12 to 462 yards and a new shaft, known as Llewellyn, was also sunk to 512 yards. In 1918 there were over a thousand men working at the Britannic, Dinas Main, Trane and Llewellyn. A PSA dated March 1926 stated that all sidings in the area were now the responsibility of Britannic Merthyr Colliery Co. Ltd. In 1936, all the pits became owned by the Powell Duffryn Associated Collieries Ltd., their first PSA being dated August 1936.

A substantial change took place in the physical layout of the sidings in the area according to the plans for 1920 and early 1930s. The 1920 plan shows a large area of sidings on the north side of the running line accessing the Britannic pit. By 1933, all the connections into the collieries are shown on the south side of the line at the south and north end of the complex, with a running loop alongside the single line. However, by 1938, there were three sidings between the 1¾ and 2 mp. shown as Top Sidings marked 'For Storage for Trane and Llewellyn Pits'. This is the final layout available.

The Trane Pit closed in November 1953 and the Britannic in 1960. With no further coal being produced in the area, the line to Gilfach Jct. was closed on 5 June 1961. All points and ground frames were taken out of use in March 1962 and the line recovered in August 1962. Since 1930, Gilfach Goch collieries had been accessed via Gellirhaidd Jct. on the line from Llantrisant; the line from Blackmill had been used for wagon storage only since the withdrawal of the passenger service in 1930. It was taken out of use completely in 1957 with a short section retained at Gellirhaidd for engines to gain access to the water column.

A view of the Gilfach passenger station looking north, taken perhaps in connection with the renaming of the station in June 1928 when it became Gilfach Goch until closure on 22 September 1930, having opened in 1881. The platform was a terminus and the stop block at the end of the head shunt for engines to run round can be seen on the left. Through lines to/from the collieries ran on the other side of the platform and there was a colliery platform north of the public station.
(Lens of Sutton)

A view southwards of the lower end of the platform with another group including the Station Master and the station nameboard Gilfach. The booking office and waiting room and signal box at the end of the platform, together with the run-round loop, can be seen. (Lens of Sutton)

An elevated view from the signal box on 23 March 1951 of the disused passenger platform and through freight lines leading to/from the collieries on the right. Though it was 21 years since the closure of the passenger service, both buildings on the passenger platform are still standing. (SLS)

A view of the disused passenger platform on 23 March 1951 showing the run-round loop and station buildings with the collieries to be seen to the north. (SLS)

Llantrisant 1076 Class 960 in a 1922 picture at Gilfach Goch, featuring some of the freight staff on duty at the time. (Lens of Sutton)

On 13 July 1957, the Stephenson Locomotive Society ran a tour of the area including Gilfach Goch and the photographs from the trip afford some excellent views of the NCB Britannic Colliery which was still in full production. The train ran into the former Colliery platform (north of former passenger station) alongside the colliery, previously owned by Powell Duffryn, the loading screens for which are seen top left and the waste tip top centre to right. (Hugh Davies Collection)

Another view of the SLS Special on 13 July 1957. The train was provided by Cathays depot with one of their auto-fitted 55XXs 5574 (not cleaned for the occasion) and two auto coaches. The view is looking up the valley showing other colliery lines and a steep incline on the right. (Ian L. Wright)

An elevated view down the valley with the train alongside the colliery platform on which SLS members congregate. The shafts of the Britannic Colliery are seen top left with the loading screens, fed with mostly wooden 10 ton wagons, on the right. (Ian L. Wright)

5208 with Breakdown Train rescuing runaway wagons from Britannic colliery on 7 August 1955. (R. Darlaston)

CHAPTER 5

LLANHARAN BRANCH

Tondu to Ynysawdre Jct. and onto the Llanharan branch at Tynycoed Jct., has already been covered in the section on Tondu Ogmore Jct. to Brynmenyn. We start this analysis of the branch at Tynycoed Jct. The Tondu to Bryncethin section was opened in 1892 to join the Llanharan to Bryncethin and on to Cardiff & Ogmore Jct. section which had opened in 1876. The line was well populated with collieries, though most had disappeared by about 1930, some being re-opened in later years as opencast sites.

Access to the line at Llanharan was removed in December 1962 but remained in use from the Tondu end for access to opencast sites. The branch re-opened after 1962 from the Tondu end to access further opencast working at Wern Tarw, with a ten-year working agreement. When the completion date arrived in 1973, the line was mothballed but re-opened in October 1977 until April 1982 for further supplies of opencast coal from Wern Tarw for Uskmouth B Power Station. The connection to the branch at Ynysawdre was taken out of use on 6 April 1984 and the recovery of all remaining trackwork was completed on 4 June 1984.

TYNYCOED JCT.

Tynycoed Jct., came into being when the line from Tondu to Bryncethin opened in 1892 and was originally known as Pencoed Jct. A plan of the junction in 1897 shows there to have been a complete triangle of lines with Tynycoed as the base point from where a south single line fork deviated to Ynysawdre Jct. then on to Tondu Ogmore Jct., and a north fork of double line track deviated to Brynmenyn Jct; the track across the top of the triangle was the line from Tondu to Brynmenyn. By 1915, the north fork from Tynycoed to Brynmenyn had been reduced to two sidings stop-blocked at the Tynycoed end, so Tynycoed was no longer a junction. The SB there was closed in about 1938.

Between Tynycoed and Bryncethin was Maendy Drift Mine with east and west connections into two loop sidings for exchange of traffic and access to further colliery sidings. In 1915 it was owned by the Maendy Colliery Co. and in 1923 produced 15,000 tons of coal with 81 miners underground. By 1927, the number employed had risen to 150 but the economics of the mine caused closure in 1930.

Ynysawdre Junction looking north with the Llanharan Branch diverging right looking towards Bryncethin on 4 August 1964. (Garth Tilt)

Ynysawdre Junction looking south towards Tondu with the Llanharan Branch converging left with the Ogmore/Garw Lines to the right. Tondu Ogmore Junction Signal Box controlled the junction and can be seen in the distance on the 6 August 1963. (Garth Tilt)

Tynycoed Junction, as seen on 6 August 1963 looking towards Bryncethin, once formed a triangle but was removed in 1915. The truncated chord was used for storage sidings accessed from Brynmenyn. (Garth Tilt)

BRYNCETHIN JCT.

Approaching the future site of Bryncethin Jct., about half a mile to the west at just under 5½ miles from Llanharan, was Bryncethin Colliery, access controlled by Bryncethin Colliery Sidings SB at 5m 34ch from Llanharan. There were many shallow drift mines in the area producing house coal from the Red Ash seam and one that was more fully developed was a mine opened by the Barrow (in Furness) Hematite Steel Co. Ltd. which wanted to exploit the more profitable steam coal seams which lay at a much greater depth. A PSA was granted to the company in

November 1876 but by 1908, the colliery was being run by the Bryncethin Colliery Co. Ltd., the Barrow Nos 2 and 3 pits employing some 200 men. The colliery closed at the end of 1915, re-opened as the New Bryncethin but closed again in 1921.

A plan for 1897 shows the colliery sidings leading to a Bryncethin Brickworks, also owned by the Barrow Co. with a PSA dated August 1892. Two loop sidings alongside the running line were added probably in 1907 and lasted in use until January 1950, the branch to the colliery and brickworks lasting until the end of 1964, controlled from Bryncethin East GF which was taken out of use at the

This 6 August 1963 view shows the site of Tynycoed Junction looking towards Tondu. The storage sidings created after closure bear witness to their latter-day use. (Garth Tilt)

same time. This was previously called the Barrow Siding GF until 1907 when it was moved 4ch further east.

Half a mile further east was Bryncethin Jct., the deviation point for the branch to Cardiff & Ogmore Jct., opened in October 1876, aimed at providing a direct route from the Ogmore Valley Collieries to Cardiff and later Barry Docks. A plan of Bryncethin Jct. for 1881 shows that the two single lines of the Tondu and C&O Jct. routes ran parallel for almost a quarter of a mile between the 4½ and 4¾ mp with a scissors crossing and another connection forming running loops. By 1887, three sidings had been added at the east end of the junction, stop blocked at the east end, with a further two at the starting point of the branch, stop blocked at the north end, controlled by the Tynywaun GF.

A connection off these sidings into the Tynywaun and Heol Laethog Collieries is shown on a plan of the area for 1918. Tynywaun was owned in 1905 by the Cardiff & District Collieries Ltd. and was listed in 1913 as being owned by the Bridgend (Cardiff) Collieries Co. Ltd., employing 200 men working on the

No. 2 Rhondda seam, producing house and gas coal. By 1915/6 when owned by Bowens & Rowlands, it employed 300 men and in 1921 was shown as owned by the Tynywaun Colliery Co. By 1922, it employed only 120 men and ownership had passed to the Swansea Vale Spelting Co. then to the National Smelting Co. in April 1924 by which time it employed only 14. It closed in 1928 when it employed about 50 men.

Heol Laethog Colliery was also owned initially by the Cardiff & District Collieries Ltd. and employed only 10 men in 1900, working on the No. 3 Rhondda seam. By 1907, it employed 176 men and was still a going concern in 1910 when it employed over 150 but there are no further records.

There was another colliery on the branch, just north of Bryncethin. This was Llan (or Lan) Colliery on the east side of the line, the inlet and outlet being controlled by GF at the north and south ends of the complex. The colliery appears to have had a short life as the first PSA was dated November 1909 granted to the Llan Colliery Co. amended to the Llan Gas

The site of Bryncethin Junction on 6 August 1963 where the Cardiff & Ogmore Branch previously joined on the right. The Signal Box was closed on 11 February 1951 and regrettably a photograph has eluded the authors. (Garth Tilt)

4247 heads a train of Pit Props for Wern Tarw Colliery on 6 August 1963. The P Way cabin on the left is a conversion from the old Bryncethin Junction Signal Box. This was closed on 11 February 1951 and the truncated Cardiff and Ogmore Branch (seen to the right of the locomotive) recovered after years of use as a wagon storage facility when the line became disused in 1938. The private siding (closed in 1964) to Bryncethin Brickworks is a quarter mile behind the train with access controlled by a Ground Frame. 4247 emerged from Swindon works on 31 March 1916 spending most of her years allocated to Ebbw Junction. With straight frames and outside steam pipes, 4247 was withdrawn from service on the closure of Tondu shed on 18 April 1964 but happily passed into preservation and is now at work on the Bodmin & Wenford Railway in Cornwall (she was at St Blazey from 1952 to 1957). (Garth Tilt)

Coal Co. Ltd. of Bridgend in August 1910. It employed 20 men in 1913 before being closed in November 1915.

Either through lack of use or perhaps because of the cost of upkeep of the viaduct crossing the Blackmill to Hendreforgan line, the branch was closed in July 1938 but the sidings on the branch at Bryncethin were retained for wagon storage until finally taken out of use in February 1951. Bryncethin Jct. SB (originally Ty Hirwain) which would have dated back to the opening of the branch in 1876, was replaced by a new box in 1894 at 4m 51ch and remained in use until February 1951 when the sidings east of the box were also taken out of use and the location reduced to one plain line.

RAGLAN

On the approach to Raglan from Bryncethin, a plan for 1920 shows Trefach (or Drefach) colliery on the north side of the line between the 3¾ and 3½mp. It is shown as open in 1917 under the ownership of E.T. David on behalf of the Trefach Colliery Co. and in 1918 by the International Colliery Co. with a PSA to them dated November 1920, with only five men employed. It was listed as abandoned in 1921 but had been re-opened by 1924 when it employed 50 men. It was again abandoned in 1927 when it only employed four men and closed again at the end of 1929. It had been re-opened again by 1938 when it employed about 40 men, owned by Bridgend Collieries Ltd. By 1940 it employed 75 men, but low production figures caused it to close for good in February 1943. The site had been cleared by 1944. The rail layout there consisted of a loop with two sidings, stop-blocked at both ends, serving the screens with central connections between each siding and the loop. Trefach Colliery Sidings SB was shown as open in 1924 on the south side of the line at the centre of the complex.

The 1881 plan shows that between 3m 43ch and 3m 25ch there was another colliery complex called Brynwith and Cribbwr Main Colliery, two tramroad accessed collieries well north of the main line which sent their coal down to the loading screens adjacent to the main line, which would become the site of Raglan Colliery.

Brynwith was opened by Hedley's Collieries Ltd., about 1875 to work the Nos 2 and 3 Rhondda seams. It employed some 370 men in 1908 but only 19 in 1909, rising to 91 in 1913 but only 15 in 1916. Matters improved after they were taken over by the Raglan Colliery Co. in 1916 and by 1918, the pit employed over 200 men.

Cribbwr Main Colliery was opened about 1878 by the Cribbwr Main Coal & Coke Co., though there are records of a Cribbwr Colliery in the 1850's. By 1884 it had passed to Williams & Davies but had to abandon work on its Lantern seam in 1879 and 1891 and its Wern Tarw seam in 1885. In 1893, Cribbwr Main colliery was renamed the South Glamorgan Colliery but seems to have closed in 1896. A New

Cribbwr Colliery, which may well have been the same undertaking, took over but abandoned all its seams in 1908 when it appears to have closed.

Raglan Colliery was developed with sidings and screens alongside the main line in 1900 by Hedley's Colliery Co., composed of at least four different drift sections. Employing some 200 men in 1907 and 275 in 1908, this rose to over 400 in 1913 when it advertised its product through its Sales Agent as:

E. W. Cook & Co., Swansea & Cardiff
Colliery Proprietors, Coal Exporters &
Pitwood Importers
Sole Shippers of 'Primrose' and
'Hedleys' Smokeless Steam Coal
'Raglan' Gas & Bunker Coal
'Gleison' Anthracite (Big Vein)
'Tareni' Anthracite' (Red Vein)
Shipping Ports – Swansea, Cardiff,
Barry, Newport and Port Talbot
Shippers of all descriptions of Steam &
Anthracite Coals, Bunker Coals and
Patent Fuel.

In 1916, ownership passed to the Raglan Collieries Ltd., who in 1918 employed 250 men. At the end of 1926, a new Washery was built at the colliery to improve its competition in coal standards. In 1935, the losses being incurred caused the colliery to be closed but in January 1936, it was re-opened by Meiros Collieries (1931) Ltd., passing to the South Wales Coalite Co. in May 1937. The whole undertaking closed at the end of 1943 and many of the sidings were taken up.

In February 1956, the NCB re-opened the site as Raglan Opencast Disposal Centre with two long loop sidings next to the main line and various sidings leading off. The PSA to the NCB was dated March 1960 and was terminated in February 1982. Access to the site was by GF at either end. Raglan Opencast was not used for the whole of this period and was closed for an unknown period during the 1970s. It re-opened, probably with MGR working to Aberthaw Power

Station, the first train of empties arriving on 30 November 1977 and leaving on 5 December.

WERN TARW COLLIERY

Wern Tarw Colliery was located between the 2¾ and 3mp from Llanharan. A colliery existed on the site in the nineteenth century, records show a SB closing there c1899. However, the only records that exist are relative to a colliery that opened in 1907 when a PSA was granted to Cardiff & Ogmore Collieries in October. A plan of the area for 1915 shows two loop sidings north of the main line with connections leading off northwards to the colliery at the east end, access being via two GFs, one at the west end at 2m.78ch., the other at the east end at 2m.60ch. From 1915 the colliery was owned by Meiros Collieries who had a PSA from February 1916 until May 1937. The mine consisted of both drifts and pits, the latter sunk by the Meiros Co. in 1920. The colliery produced house, manufacturing and gas coals.

The colliery was taken over in 1937 by the South Wales Coalite Co., who in May 1938 installed a new layout of five long loop sidings north of the main line to replace the previous layout with a siding to the colliery as before at the east end and connections with the main line by ground frames, both shown as brought into use in 1938, between 2m.59ch. at the east end and 3m.15ch. at the west. The east end GF was taken out of use in November 1966, but the west end remained in use to service the sidings until October 1973, the site having closed at the end of 1972. It was however re-opened and was the last opencast site working in the area in 1982.

On 15 February 1979, 37178 propels its Inspection Saloon towards Wern Tarw. Fortunately, the steam heating is working well on what was evidently a cold day. (Stuart Warr)

SOUTH RHONDDA COLLIERY

Between the 1¼ and 1½mp from Llanharan, until 1928-30, there were significant colliery establishments in the area of South Rhondda SB, which closed in 1899 with GF facilities thereafter. A plan of the area for 1891 shows two loop sidings alongside the main line to which South Rhondda SB was central on the south side of the running line. A connection from the west end of these sidings led to the Llanbad Colliery, opened by the Llanbad Colliery Co. in 1884 only to be abandoned a few years later.

In 1891 it was restarted as the South Rhondda Colliery by Daniel Owen, producing coal and fireclay, passing to the South Rhondda Colliery Co. Ltd. in August 1893, then to the South Rhondda Co. (1898) Ltd. with effect from January 1899. In 1910, a new pit was sunk adjacent to the South Rhondda. At its peak in 1914, the colliery employed 450 men, but this reduced until in 1923 there were only just over 200 and the colliery closed in 1927, as did an adjoining brickworks, where the fireclay was used. In about 1955, three small drift mines were opened at Llanbad, producing just over 5,000 tons of coal in 1960 but they closed in 1964 and were abandoned in 1966. Adjoining the branch line to the colliery there was a one-track Goods shed and yard, known as South Rhondda Goods which opened in April 1918 and closed on 1 January 1930.

Also accessed from the west end of the complex was Cwm Ciwc Colliery. A loop on the north side of the running line between Cwm Ciwc East and West GFs, operational between 1910-28, accessed a long branch to Cwm Ciwc, the first PSA granted to South Rhondda Collieries Co. (1898) Ltd. in 1907 and passing in May 1909 to the Gas Coal Collieries Ltd., then to Meiros Collieries Ltd. in July 1914 who owned the colliery until closure in July 1928.

After the closure of South Rhondda Goods, preceded by that of the collieries, all sidings and connections in the area were removed between 1928-30 and the area became plain line.

LLANHARAN

The Cardiff & Ogmore branch, built by David Davies to provide direct access for his coal from the Ogmore Valleys to Cardiff Docks, was opened in 1876, leaving the SWML just east of the station at what was then called Llanharan West Junction SB, the Junction being dropped by 1890. There was a 20ch. loop at which trains could wait for access to either the main line or branch on which a Colliers Platform was sited between 1890-97. The last train to use the Llanharan section of the branch ran on 10 February 1962 and the branch was closed on 3 December 1962, the junction having been taken out on the previous day.

Llanharan looking west c1952 on the Down Main Line with the Goods Loops to the left and Goods yard on the extreme left. Beyond the road bridge the double track of the Ogmore Branch can be seen diverging off to the right. The junction was closed on 3 December 1962 and the line as far as Wern Tarw accessed from Tondu Ogmore Junction. (P.J. Garland/R.S. Carpenter)

CHAPTER 6

ENTHUSIAST SPECIALS

A number of Enthusiast Specials have visited the Tondu Valleys as part of their itineraries. A brief summary of these is included here along with some illustrations. The website (www.sixbellsjunction.co.uk) provides comprehensive details of these and others (including actual Timings) that have operated throughout Great Britain. Readers wishing to obtain more information are invited to refer to this trove. Thanks are also expressed to Gary Thornton for allowing us to extract some of the information to fill gaps in our research.

Note-The Vale of Glamorgan line is abbreviated VoG.

Extract from the 1955 Working Timetable showing (inter alia) Engine Loads for Excursion trains.

Engine Loads for Passenger, Parcels, Milk and Fish Trains for Engine Working Purposes—continued   G111

LOADS FOR RAIL MOTOR ENGINES

Gradient	0-4-2 T Tons	0-6-0 T Tons
1-40	72	90
1-50	96	120
1-60	120	150
1-80	144	180
1-100	168	210

The tonnage loads shewn in the "Engine Loads Table" do not apply when Rail Motor services are being worked by engines of the 14XX, 54XX and 64XX classes, the authorised loads for which are specially laid down separately, in accordance with the instructions in the General Appendix.

LOADS OF PASSENGER TRAINS—SCHOOL PARTIES SPECIALS, RHONDDA VALLEY STATIONS TO PORTHCAWL, via CYMMER AFAN

SECTION From	To	B.R. Standard Class 4 75XXX and 76XXX 41XX, 51XX, 61XX, 53XX, 63XX, 73XX, 56XX, 66XX Tons	0-6-2T "C" Group Tons	B.R. Standard Class 3 45XX 55XX 36XX, 37XX, 46XX, 57XX, 77XX, 34XX, 84XX, 94XX, 87XX, 96XX, 97XX Tons	B.R. Standard Class 2 22XX, 32XX Tons	0-6-0T "A" Group Tons
Treherbert	Cymmer Afan	200	145	140	130	115
Cymmer Afan	Treherbert	200	145	140	130	115
Cymmer Afan	Porthcawl	200	145	140	130	115
Porthcawl	Cymmer Afan	200	145	140	130	115

These loads to apply for through Excursions only. The loads set out under the "D" Group heading are for 56XX and 66XX engines only.

POINT-TO-POINT TIMES FOR ABOVE LOADS

UP TRAINS		
Cymmer Afan to Tondu (pass)	25 minutes	This timing to apply in both directions and to through excursion trains only.
Tondu to Pyle (pass)	14 "	
Pyle to Porthcawl	11 "	

LOADS OF EMPTY PASSENGER STOCK TRAINS, FERNDALE BRANCH

From	To	56XX and 66XX Engines Tons	0-6-2T "C" Group Tons	0-6-0T "A" Group Tons	Special conditions respecting timing, etc., if any
Porth	Ferndale	198	145	125	21 minutes
Ferndale	Maerdy	198	145	100	11 minutes

EXCEPTIONAL LOADS FOR EXCURSION AND SPECIAL PASSENGER TRAINS—NELSON & LLANCAIACH AND DOWLAIS (CAE HARRIS)

	56XX Class 66XX Class Tons	Group "A" Tons	0-6-2T "C" Group Tons
Nelson & Llancaiach to Bedlinog	170*	110*	120*
Bedlinog to Dowlais (Cae Harris)	160*	105*	115*
Dowlais (Cae Harris) to Nelson & Llancaiach	220	160	170

*—Additional running time required.
Special trains from Cardiff, Barry or Newport direction to take water at Llanbradach to avoid stopping at Ffaldcaiach or Nantyffyn.

SPECIAL LOADS FOR THROUGH LONDON EXPRESS TRAINS, ETC., DIVERTED IN CASE OF EMERGENCY, to run between Cardiff (General) and Pengam Sidings via Roath Branch Junction and Docks Storage North, also via Cardiff (Queen St.) and Stonefield Junction.

From	To	50XX etc. Tons	49XX etc. Tons	0-6-2 T etc. Tons	0-6-0 etc. Tons
Cardiff (General)	Pengam Sidings	455	406	352	252
Pengam Sidings	Cardiff (General)				

SPECIAL LOADS FOR PASSENGER TRAINS DIVERTED IN CASE OF EMERGENCY VIA ROUTES NOT NORMALLY USED FOR PASSENGER TRAIN WORKING

SECTION From	To	4074, etc. Tons	49XX, etc. Tons	45XX, etc. Tons	0-6-0, etc. Tons	14XX, etc. Tons
Llanharan West (Via Tondu and Waterhall Jn.)	Margam Junction	394	336	288	240	200
Llanharan West (Via Tondu)	Pyle	394	336	288	240	200
Llanharan West (Via Tondu)	Bridgend	436	336	288	240	200
Margam Junction (Via Waterhall Junction and Tondu)	Llanharan West	326	288	224	196	164
Pyle (Via Tondu)	Llanharan West	326	288	224	196	164
Bridgend (Via Tondu)	Llanharan West	326	288	224	196	164

12 July 1952 South Wales Mineral Lines 6423 + 2 x Taff Vale Auto Trailers
Cardiff General Ninian Park Waterhall Jct (reverse) Common Branch Jct Cross Inn Llantrisant Ogmore Jct (reverse) Tonteg Jct Pontypridd Rhondda Cutting Cilfynydd Upper Boat Penrhos Jct Walnut Tree Jct Tynycaeau Jct St Fagans Cardiff

Having reversed at Ogmore Junction, the special retraces its path back to Llanharan. The wagons on the left are empties for supply to collieries on those branches and were used as an overflow for Ogmore Yard. (R.C. Riley/Transport Treasury)

29 May 1954 Port Talbot Railway Tour Stephenson Locomotive Society
3680 5734 8740 + 2 x LMS Corridor Coaches
Bridgend Cowbridge Road Coity Jct Tondu (reverse) Cefn Margam Yard Duffryn Jct Bryn Cwmdu Aberavon Town Tonmawr Jct Port Talbot Bridgend.

The special traversed the former Port Talbot Railway. Their line to Pontyrhyll was closed to passengers on 12 September 1932, the line eventually being truncated at Cwmdu (recorded here) where a connection gave access to St. John's Colliery. In September 1964, the line from Cwmdu to Llynvi Junction was transferred into NCB ownership. (D.K. Jones Collection)

26 June 1955 South Wales Diesel Railcar Tour RCTS AEC Railcar W23.
Bristol Tondu OVE Neath & return (outward on the 25th, returning on the 26th)
Certainly this was the only occasion one of these handsome machines visited Tondu.

The DRC tour is first seen at the Up Porthcawl platform where it has arrived from Neath, and then awaits departure from the Up Main platform for Bridgend. (RCTS)

2 July 1960 South Wales Tour Stephenson Locomotive Society (Midland Area)
Auto Train W192 6416 W245 W175 Bridgend / Caerau / Cardiff
9634 + 1921 Main Line & City Stock W3756 W3910 W3755 Caerau & North Rhondda
Arguably, this was the most comprehensive special embracing the Tondu Valleys
network. A number of additional illustrations offer views to support some of the location
details. The actual itinerary was;

Bridgend Cowbridge Road (reverse) Coity Jct Blaengarw Brynmenyn (reverse)
Nantymoel (reverse) Tondu (reverse) Caerau (change trains) Caerau North Rhondda
Halt (propelled from Caerau) & Return (change trains) Abergwynfi (reverse) Llantrisant
via Tondu North Curve, Llanharan Llantrisant (reverse) Penygraig (reverse) Cardiff.

The special is shown here in Bridgend's Barry Bay at the start of its itinerary. This began with a move to Cowbridge Road Junction, then traversing the former Barry Railway route to Coity Junction. The second view is at Brynmenyn before proceeding to Nantymoel.

8 June 1963 Mid Glamorgan Railtour West Glamorgan Rly. Soc./Monmouthshire Rly. Soc.
6435 + Autos W241 W242.
Bridgend Blaengwynfi Porthcawl Swansea via SDL & Felin Fran return to Tondu via SDL
and OVE.

The train is seen here at Tondu on its outward journey to Blaengwynfi.

21 November 1964 Y Ddraig Goch Swansea Railway Circle
9678 + 3 Coaches of Corridor Stock.
Neath Abergwynfi Glyncorrwg Tondu Blaengarw (propelled from Pontycymmer)
Brynmenyn Nantymoel Swansea High St.

The last steam-hauled railtour of the Tondu Valleys, this shot shows the special arriving at Tondu on the first leg of its journey and affords a good appreciation of Tondu Middle as 9678 takes a well-earned drink. The next will be at Abergwynfi.

14 October 1967 South Wales Railtour Nº1 Warwickshire Rly Soc. Class 120 3 x Car Unit Newport Machen Caerphilly Aber Penrhos Walnut Tree Jct Stormstown Lady Windsor Colliery Pontypridd Treherbert Cymmer Maesteg Blaengarw Nantymoel Wern Tarw Tondu VoG and Cardiff.

The DMU is seen at Brynmenyn having just returned from the Garw Valley, and is about to draw forward to reverse into the Ogmore platform before proceeding to Nantymoel. At this time Brynmenyn had been substantially reduced to a basic junction.

19 October 1968 South Wales Tour Enthusiast Club Class 120 3 x Car Unit Pontypridd Cymmer Tondu Blaengarw Brynmenyn Nantymoel Ogmore Jct Wern Tarw Bridgend.

The DMU is seen running into Tondu's former Porthcawl platform, showing the footbridge and the former engine shed which is still intact.

3 July 1971 Dulais & Llynfi Valleys Railtour Branch Line Society
DMU 50091 59041 50133
Cardiff Llynfi Jct Tondu OVE Port Tennant Jct Upper Bank Morriston East Llansamlet
(Six Pit) Burrows Jct Craig-y-Nos Jersey Marine Jct South Neath Canalside Court Sart
Tondu Wern Tarw Tondu Bridgend VoG Cardiff.
Llynfi Jct Cwmdu Nantyffyllon Llynfi Jct preserved 9642 on NCB Lines.

The special stands on the Porthcawl side of the Tondu layout with empty 'Hyfits' alongside for timber traffic from Corpach to Bridgend Paper Mills at Gelli Las.

The 3car DMU stands in the Valley platform (4) at Bridgend after arrival from Cardiff.

At Llynfi Jct. with restored pannier 9642 about to propel wagons of members onto NCB tracks.

At Cefn Junction the special takes the OVE on route to Swansea Docks.

28 April 1973 Llynfi & Ogmore Dean Forest RPS Class 120 3 x Car Unit
Gloucester Barry Pier VoG Bridgend Llynfi Jct Tondu Nantymoel Blaengarw Cefn Pyle
Margam Abbey East & return Tondu Bridgend Cardiff Gloucester.

A Llynvi Jct the preserved 9642 conveyed the group to Cwmdu along the remnants of
the former North's Navigation and PTR at that time operated by the NCB. Interestingly
the couplings were lengthened and corridor connections disconnected between Cefn and
Pyle due to the curvature.

The DMU tour pauses at Tondu. (R.K. Blencowe)

21 January 1979 Welsh Wizard R.P.P.R. 37228 (to Cardiff) 50008 37286 (from Cardiff) Paddington to Tondu via VoG Margam Burrows Sidings Onllwyn Briton Ferry Swansea Paddington.

The special arrives at Tondu and is about to draw forward onto the Maesteg line then reverse into the Porthcawl Loop in order to run round. Despite the coating of snow, the onlookers' attire suggests it's a mild day. (Stuart Warr)

37186 enters the Porthcawl loop at Tondu in order to reverse and head for the Garw or Ogmore leg of its journey, 33019 is at the other end. The site of Velin Vach Signal Box is behind 37186 and to the right, access to Velin Vach yard.

28 September 1985 Welsh Washery Wanderer Hertfordshire Railtours 33019 37176 45139 Paddington Rose Heyworth Barry Island Cardiff Tondu via Penarth Curve Maesteg Blaengarw Ogmore Vale Washery Cefn Margam Paddington.

26 September 1992 DME Demise Monmouthshire Railway Society
C392 (51147 51134) + C395 (51140 51133)
Newport VoG Ford Sidings Burrows Sidings Onllwyn Burrows Sidings Margam Port
Talbot Docks Iron Ore Terminal Newlands Blaengarw Tondu Cardiff.

The 4-car formation is approaching Tondu and destined for Blaengarw.

28 March 2009 Cwm & Go(ne) Pathfinder Railtours 37401 60024
Nottingham Margam Newlands Tondu Bridgend VoG Cardiff Machen Quarry
Uskmouth Nottingham.

The train just west of Kenfig Hill with 374021 on the
rear. (Mark Thomas)

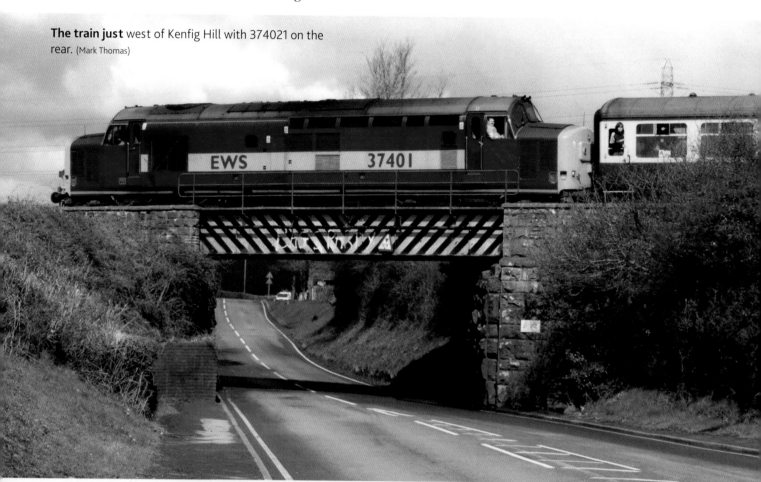

**The train
approaching** Tondu
with 60024 leading.
(Mark Thomas)

37401 on the rear as the train draws onto the Garw Branch to reverse before heading along the line to Bridgend. (Mark Thomas)

13 June 2009 The Thames Towy UK Railtours 59205 59206
Paddington Cockett Carmarthen Felin Fran Newlands Tondu VoG Paddington.
Three round trips steam hauled on the Gwili Railway was included.

The *Thames Towy*
approaches Tondu
from Carmarthen with
59205 leading and
59206 trailing.

59206 bringing up
the rear ventures onto
the Garw Branch in
order to reverse, then
head the formation to
Paddington.

24 March 2012 Coal Grinder Pathfinder Railtours 37603 37606 66304
Crewe Birmingham Bristol Parkway Llynvi Jct Newlands Margam Cockett Llanelli
Gwaun-Cae-Gurwen Burrows Sidings Cwmgwrach Jersey Marine Bristol Parkway
Birmingham Crewe.

The *Coal Grinder* heads out of Tondu bound for Margam with 66304 in charge. (Phil Trotter)

24 August 2014 Taffy Tug (2) Pathfinder Railtours 60039 60040
Bristol (TM) VoG Briton ferry Newlands Maesteg Bridgend Aberdare Tower Colliery
Bristol.

The *Taffy Tug* stands in the Llynvi Valley refuge with 60039 in rear. (Stephen Miles)

The **Driver of** 60039 exchanges Tokens at Tondu on the return from Maesteg on route to Aberdare. (Stephen Miles)

Deep in the jungle at Cwmffos between Cefn Junction and Tondu illustrating the condition of the line now that scheduled train movements are minimal. (Stephen Miles)

CHAPTER 7

MAIN LINE DIVERSIONS

The two southern sections of the former Tondu Valleys network provide an alternative to the South Wales Mainline between Bridgend and Port Talbot when this is closed. The individual routes are single, permissible line speeds are restrictive and the need to reverse at Tondu all increase the overall transit time which in turn places capacity at a premium. For these reasons, in 2004 it was considered no longer viable to divert passenger trains this way and buses are used to replace passenger trains when the main line is closed. However, the streamlining of steel processing results in the inter-works rail movements forming a critical and integral part of the production line. In this case, the Tondu route remains essential and the following images record some occasions when this has been employed.

On Sunday 27 July 1980, the main line was closed for planned engineering work with all trains scheduled via Tondu.

A Main Line Diversion on 27 July 1980. The 0815 Paddington to Swansea approaches Tondu from Bridgend.
(Stuart Warr)

(Top Left) **The train runs** onto the Llynvi line where the Driver changes ends and (top right) receives the Token for the single line to Margam. The train then runs forward into the former Porthcawl platform at Tondu where it meets the 1010 Swansea to Paddington (bottom) which has already arrived in the Up Branch loop and in clear, surrendered the Token. It then waits for the down train to clear the Down Loop on its way to Margam before it also draws forward onto the Llynvi line, reverses then continues to Bridgend and on to Paddington. (Stuart Warr)

On a previous diversion on 23 September 1979, the 0845 (Sun) Swansea to Paddington comes off the line from Margam at Tondu and will run to Tondu Middle to reverse onto the line to Bridgend. (Stuart Warr)

On the line from Margam, 47 080 heading the Carmarthen to Reading Premium Parcels out of the Up Branch Loop on a 30 November 1979 diversion. (Stuart Warr)

A landslip at Mawdlam caused a two-week closure of the South Wales mainline in November 1979. To avoid running round at Tondu trains were provided with locomotives at both ends. These views taken on the 30th capture the scene;

Also on 30th November 1979, On 37239 & 37186 convey a train of Western Valley coal for Margam seen arriving at Tondu alongside the Down Llynvi platform then past Tondu Middle Signal Box before reversing. (Stuart Warr)

Also on 30th November 1979 diversion, 47128 & 47185 with 37186 in rear bring a train of empty oil tanks up from Bridgend destined for Milford Haven. (Stuart Warr)

Due to planned engineering work either side of Bridgend for a number of Sundays in January 2012, Freight was diverted via Tondu and then the Vale of Glamorgan whilst Passengers were conveyed by road. These views are on 15 January 2012.

On a freight diversion on 15 January 2012, 60054 heads 6M41 the 10.41 Margam to Round Oak into Tondu and reverses via the Garw Branch. (Stuart Warr)

60054 has reversed on the Garw branch and now takes the line to Bridgend on 15 January 2012. (S. Warr)

A long lapse arises before another spate of diversions took place in January 2015. All images were taken on 11 January.

On 11 January 2015, 66056 approaches Coity Junction through Litchard with the 11.14 Margam to Middlesbrough. (Stephen Miles)

On the same occasion, 66187 with 6O32 0857 Margam to Llanwern arrives at Tondu, then, after reversing on the Garw branch, heads for Bridgend. (Stuart Warr)

66187 in the process of running round the 0857 Margam to Dollands Moor on 11th January 2015, viewed from the footbridge and approaches one of Tondu's fine twin bracket Lower Quadrant Semaphores. (Stephen Miles)

Also on 11 January 2015, 66199 in charge of 6B66 the 0843 Llanwern to Margam Steel Coil empties heads along the line from Bridgend.
(Stephen Miles)

Again on 11 January 2015, 66082 hauls 6E30 1325 (Sun) Margam to Hartlepool on the line from Margam into the Down branch loop at Tondu, proceeds onto the Garw branch in order to run round, then comes off the Garw Branch and moves onto the Bridgend line.
(Stephen Miles)

CHAPTER 8

CHRONOLOGIES

Saturday 7 July 1962 Tondu to Porthcawl

On Saturday 7 July 1962, Sid Rickard travelled from his home in Cardiff to visit Bridgend, Tondu and the Porthcawl branch on one of his days touring areas of South Wales and recording the railway scene. This section shows most of the photographs he took that day. Sid's photographs are now held in the J&J Collection owned by Keith Jones of Mountain Ash and Malcolm James of Rogerstone.

11.15am Adding flavour to the warm sunny day, Radyr's 4160 runs through Bridgend with 2Z30 9.30am Rhymney to Porthcawl excursion run on behalf of Sunday Schools in the Rhymney Valley, the five carriages conveying 200 adults and 250 children. This engine is now preserved at the West Somerset Railway.

11.20am 9649 stands at the Branch platform 4 with the two-coach train for Blaengwynfi. The 7.55am Neyland to Paddington is in the Up Main platform. Note the engine carrying the new 88H shedplate which replaced 86F.

11.25am 9649 departs for Blaengwynfi.

12.15pm 4967 Shirenewton Hall had recently been reallocated from 83C Exeter to 87A Neath and is seen here, in quite clean condition, running past Bridgend Goods into the station with the 11.5am Swansea (High Street) to Weston-super-Mare running approximately 10 minutes late. In good enough condition for express work, 4967 would be condemned two months later.

12.20pm 5208 Approaches Bridgend with the 12.10pm Tondu to Pengam Class H freight. As the 11.05am Swansea to Manchester was running late and occupying the Up Main Platform, 5208 has been routed this way allowing the Signalman to clear the section in rear and accept the 12.10pm from Tondu due Bridgend at 12.26pm (hauled by 4121). This then formed the 12.45pm to Blaengwynfi. Clearly Bridgend Middle Signalman using the layout to maximum benefit. The high level of Freight trains even encroached on busy Summer Saturdays and the South Wales Main Line was working to a high intensity with little margin for contingencies.

12.30pm 4121 with the 12.45pm for Blaengwynfi. The crew take the opportunity to have a chat on the platform in the sunshine, as a young trainspotter has a look around 4121's cab.

12.35pm 6319 of St. Philip's Marsh arriving at Bridgend with the five-coach 9.55am Weston-super-Mare to Porthcawl express service, reporting number T24. The return working was the 2.10pm Porthcawl - Cardiff. Summer Saturday services such as this were a regular feature on the Porthcawl branch and the origin of this particular service varied each year; at one time, it came from Ilfracombe, a journey taking almost five hours, but whose lighthouse at night can be clearly seen from Porthcawl's promenade.

12.56pm 4121 passing Tondu Middle Box with the 12.45pm Bridgend to Blaengwynfi, viewed from the footbridge. Ahead, 9660 with safety valves simmering bunker first is in the Runaway Siding. She is the No. 3 North End Pilot which was continuous from 05.00 Monday to 20.00 Saturday with a loaded mineral train, (Target U2 11.00am Caerau to Tondu arriving at 12.30pm) which has been stabled for the weekend. Standing light engine alongside Tondu Shed is Duffryn Yard's 42XX 2-8-0T 5229 waiting a path home after working two (SO) trips from Margam Yard with empties. Local instructions required Tank Engines from the Neath District not to be turned at Tondu. 4121 was withdrawn in May 1965 but would happily pass into preservation.

1.10pm Having crossed 4121 at Llangynwyd at 1.05pm, 9649 approaches Tondu, bunker first, with the return 12.40pm Blaengwynfi to Bridgend due Tondu at 1.12pm, 5229 still remains adjacent to the engine shed waiting to go home but likely to get the road and precede the Porthcawl passenger which is due away at 1.55pm. A loaded mineral train (U4 from Pontycymmer) has also arrived on the Down Ogmore Line.

1.12pm Seen from the footbridge, 9649 departs from Tondu bunker first with South Yard in the distance unusually bereft of any wagons.

1.35pm 9660, a long term Tondu engine, being held by signals waits to return the brakevan off U2 to the Ogmore Yard, her work for the day ending at 8pm. By contrast to the left, 6431 moves gently off shed, her work for the day has only just started. 9660 was withdrawn from Neath in November 1964 and 6431 from Tondu in January 1963.

1.36pm At Tondu North Junction, now on the Up Main, 6431 moves bunker first towards the station.

1.37pm 6431 proceeds and, having cleared the North Junction, 9660 is about to get the signal and remove U2's brake van for stabling for the weekend. Other engines are visible on Tondu Shed in the background.

1.42pm Opposite Velin Vach Signal Box (the Signal Box nameplates were cast at Reading and explains why English Vs have replaced Welsh Fs), 6431 has collected one Auto Trailer from the headshunt of Velin Vach Yard. 6410 (No. 5 Pilot) stands at the outlet of the Porthcawl Bay Platform to the left, this engine was soon to be withdrawn in November 1962 from Tondu.

1.44pm The shunter clings to the handrails of 6431 as they approach Tondu Station with the single trailer W246W in tow whilst 6410 now stands alongside. Notwithstanding the benefits of Auto working, the palaver in sandwiching the locomotive between the trailers when more than two are required, is easily overlooked.

1.45pm 6431 about to couple up to two other Auto Trailers (W245W & W256W) placed in the platform by 6410 (No. 5 Pilot) whilst 6431 collected Trailer W246W. The resistance of the mechanical rodding for control purposes between locomotive and trailers precluded more than two each end of the locomotive.

1.55pm 6431 stands at Tondu Station with the three coach auto train for Porthcawl, W246W leading with W245W and W256W trailing. The Driver operated the train from the leading Auto Trailer whilst the Fireman maintained steam on the Locomotive; A formation such as this meant a lonely shift for both.

2.04pm the train approaching Cefn Junction where the Token for the single line section Velin Vach to Cefn Junction would be exchanged for that for Cefn Junction to Pyle. The Junction gave access to Pyle (the original Llynvi & Ogmore Line) or to Margam on the Port Talbot Railway's Ogmore Vale Extension Line. In addition, a passing Loop was provided.

2.05pm Waiting to return home empty handed 4251 and Brake Van held at Cefn Junction on target U19 (1215 Tondu Porthcawl Margam). The brakevan (W17488) must be a classic example of the Western's propensity to stencil rolling stock. In addition to its allocated depot '*Bristol T.M.*' and prerequisite '*Not in Common Use*' it has the additional branding '*To work the 12.25 A.M. (SX) & SUNDAYS BRISTOL T.M. To CARMARTHEN JUNCTION and 09.10 P.M. CARMARTHEN JUNCTION To BRISTOL E.D. (SO) T.M. (SX).*' So much for the restricted use and branding!

2.08pm Approaching Kenfig Hill, the Level Crossing can just be seen.

2.18pm Heol-y-Sheet Crossing Signal Box. The double track line curving away to the left was from Pyle West giving direct access onto the Porthcawl Branch from Swansea avoiding the need to reverse at Pyle. Although laid out before the Second World War it was not brought into use until 15 September 1946.

2.22pm Having deposited a supply of empties at Cornelly Sidings working Target U14, 7762 and Brakevan were scheduled to return to Tondu at 2.30pm. Quarrying of the Pant Mawr Ridge at Cornelly has been a long-standing industry, latterly developed on a large scale to provide Limestone for Port Talbot Steelworks, and was the main source of originating traffic on the branch.

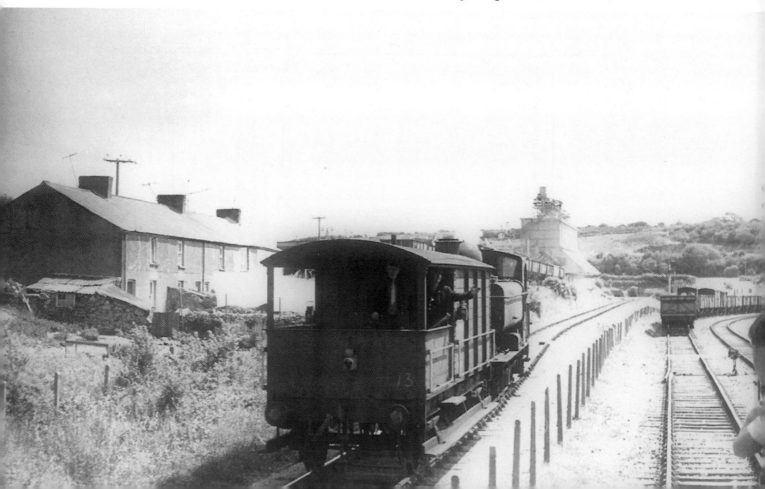

2.24pm A passing view of Nottage Halt originally named Porthcawl Golfers' Platform. Passengers wishing to alight needed to inform the guard at the previous stopping point and those wishing to join needed to provide the Driver with an indication to stop.

2.26pm As the 1.55pm from Tondu approaches its destination, 4160 with the stock of 2Z30, the Rhymney Sunday School excursion, awaits time for the return journey in the sidings.

2.27pm 6431 enters platform 1 at Porthcawl.

2.28pm Having come to a stand, the passengers detrain. Trailer W256W nearest the camera.

3.09pm The same train (6431 and the three Auto Trailers) is now ready for departure with a service to Pyle. Taken from the buffer-stops, the view shows all the station and the water tower beyond.

3.19pm Perhaps to avoid the hurly-burly of holidaymakers and Sunday School trippers, the intrepid photographer has re-joined the Porthcawl-Pyle auto train providing this view of the approach to Pyle with the A48 Trunk Road overbridge.

3.21pm 6431 stands at Pyle, its train crew and station staff chatting in the sunshine.

3.25pm 6431 departs from Pyle making use of the double track section to Cornelly. Together, the entourage will make five more round trips: Then at 9.15pm set off with the last departure of the day from Porthcawl (this time main line to Bridgend rather than Tondu) and work the 10.25pm to Cymmer before returning home from there empty stock.

Saturday 3 May 1958 Last Passenger Services to Nantymoel

Saturday 3 May 1958 saw the end of Passenger services to Nantymoel. Sid Rickard and his friend Bob Tuck were in the area to record the final day's working, with others also on the scene.

Note - Negatives by Sid Rickard are now held in the D.K. Jones J & J Collection and those by R.O. Tuck in the Rail Archive Stephenson, with prints held by Michael J. Back

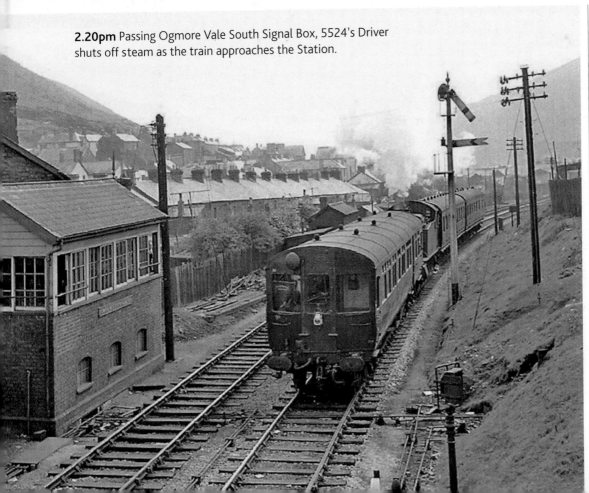

2.20pm Passing Ogmore Vale South Signal Box, 5524's Driver shuts off steam as the train approaches the Station.

2.14pm This is the 1.55pm Bridgend to Nantymoel which was the last working of the second morning turn which consisted of two round trips to Nantymoel by 5524. The engine is seen here departing from Blackmill with the tall Blackmill Junction Signal Box adjacent to the platform. In true Auto mode, 5524 is sandwiched between W171W leading, intermediate trailer W1695W and W256W trailing.

2.21pm 5524 at Ogmore Vale, the commercial centre of the Ogmore Valley. The building immediately behind W171W is the Gwalia General Ironmongers Store now preserved at the Welsh Folk Museum at St Fagans. (R.O. Tuck/Rail Archive Stephenson)

2.22pm Seen from the footbridge at the south end of the station, given the right away on the gradient rising of 1:41, 5524 departs from Ogmore Vale towards Nantymoel with the North Box to the right where track connections giving access to Aber Colliery and the Goods Shed opposite which a wagon from Bridgend Goods is seen standing alongside. Goods sundries traffic was delivered by road from Bridgend from the mid-1960s.

2.28pm 5524 approaching Nantymoel with the auto train from Bridgend, passing the large water tower. Two coaches normally sufficed on the Ogmore branch but a third trailer was added for this, the last day.

2.29pm For token exchange, the General Appendix required Drivers to reduce speed to 10 M.P.H. As 5524 draws forward, the fireman is getting ready to hand over the single line token to the signalman at Nantymoel. Downhill with 600 tons of unbraked loaded Mineral wagons in tow, such level of correctness was not always achieved. At Blackmill many a time the surrendered token had to be retrieved out of the river and the train eventually brought to a stand in order for the Fireman to walk back and pick up the token for the section to Brynmenyn that he had failed to catch, due to excess speed.

2.30pm The token now handed over, there is a final flourish from the engine for the brief 1:27 on the immediate approach to the terminus at Nantymoel.

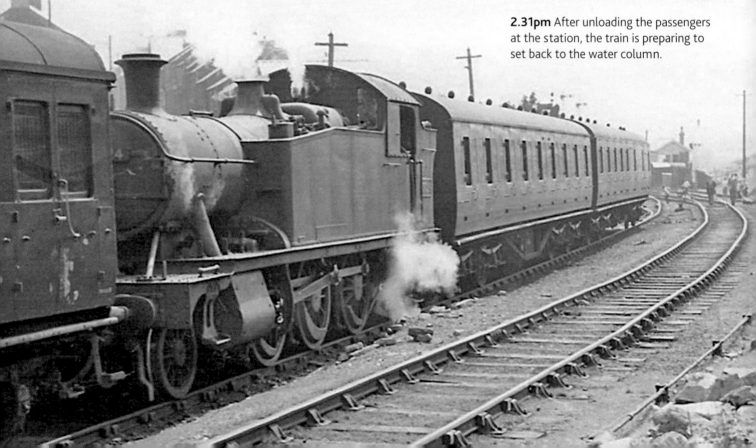

2.31pm After unloading the passengers at the station, the train is preparing to set back to the water column.

2.32pm 5524 quenches her thirst. Terraced houses form a typical backdrop.

2.42pm 5524 refreshed, is ready for the return service, the 2.45pm Nantymoel to Bridgend, downhill all the way to Bridgend.

NANTYMOEL.

2.43pm With trailer W256W now leading the formation 5524 is hidden but the Driver enjoys a brief spell on the platform seat. (R.O. Tuck/Rail Archive Stephenson)

2.44pm Five lads look on at a scene that is about to disappear forever but obviously haven't told the dog.

2.45pm 5524 awaits departure with the competition in the form of a Western Welsh Leyland Tiger Cub lurking in the background. (R.O. Tuck/Rail Archive Stephenson)

2.48pm The Signalman gets ready to exchange tokens at Wyndham Pits Signal Box. The appearance of double track is misleading; the main line was single and the adjacent line was the access loop into Wyndham Colliery. (R O Tuck/Rail Archive Stephenson)

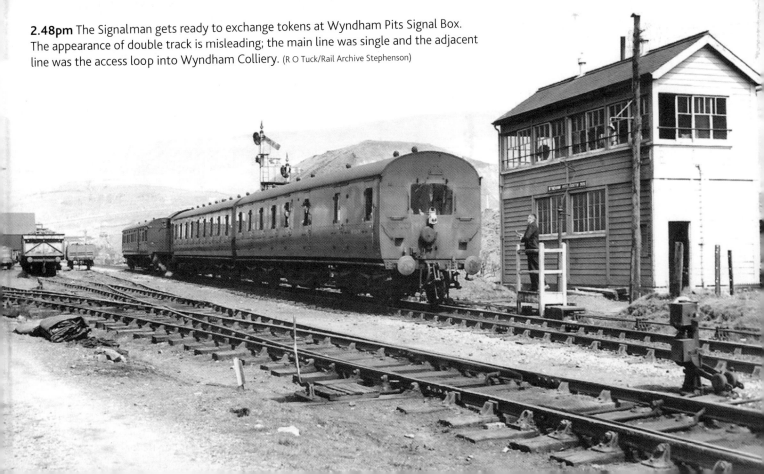

2.49pm Collecting the token at Wyndham Pits South Signal Box. Bob Tuck also records the scene. From 1935 to 1954 this type of operation was referred to as 'Auto' in the Working Timetables but the Western Region then abandoned this in favour of 'Rail Motor' The GWR however, had said farewell to proper Railmotors (a coach with an integral steam powered bogie) in 1935.

3.00pm 5524 sets off from Blackmill. She was regarded as the Ogmore Passenger engine and her next turn was a round trip to Abergwynfi before returning to the Ogmore; fittingly working the very last train from Bridgend at 11.20pm again in Auto fashion W171 in front and auto conversions 1695 and 255 behind, the driver was William Morgan. (R.O. Tuck/Rail Archive Stephenson)

3.01pm Just south of Blackmill, next stop Brynmenyn at 3.04pm. Sadly, this was the last day of passenger services on the Ogmore branch; with the reduction in Auto-fitted locomotives required at Tondu, 5524 was reallocated to Exeter in September and withdrawn from there in June 1960.

3.58pm 8497 approaches Brynmenyn with the three-coach 3.50pm Bridgend-Nantymoel. The small Ground Frame visible to the right controlled access to three sidings, the truncated remains of the chord linking with the Llanharan branch.

3.59pm Brynmenyn seen from the 3.50pm from Bridgend looking down both sides of the station building and the Level Crossing on the Garw branch. This was the first of four round trips to Nantymoel of the afternoon turns but the only one programmed for conventional (non-Auto) working. 8497 and her coaches would then work the late afternoon Porthcawl services. (D Lawrence)

4.00pm 8497 draws into the Down Ogmore Platform at Brynmenyn with W4423 W1424 and W383. (R.O. Tuck/Rail Archive Stephenson)

4.05pm Blackmill looking towards Tondu taken from rear of the train. (D Lawrence)

4.29pm 8497 at Nantymoel with the 4.30pm Nantymoel to Bridgend. The station was used during the filming of the popular comedy 'Run for your Money.' The film, directed by Charles Frend starred Donald Houston, Meredith Edwards, Moira Lister, Alec Guinness and Joyce Grenfell. It was based on the bi-annual rugby migration from South Wales to Twickenham. (E T Gill)

4.37pm 8497 pauses at Ogmore Vale with the 4.30pm Nantymoel to Bridgend. The wagons in the siding behind the platform are serving Penllwyngwent Colliery. Despite the fact this was the last day of Passenger Operation, an Excursion to Porthcawl was programmed. This departed Nantymoel at 1030, ran non-stop after Blackmill stopping only for water at Tondu and returned from Porthcawl at 7pm. The train was formed of 9 coaches (9108 2630 453 1200 473 2828 4046 1696 6226) 9108 was a Special Brake Saloon and had been based at Tondu for some time. The train was double headed by Panniers 7725 and 7753 which on arrival at Porthcawl, stabled the stock and returned light engines to Tondu, reversing the process in the late afternoon.

INDEX

Principal References & Images are in bold

Locations